MY VERY LAST BOOK
UNLESS I WRITE ANOTHER

C.J. Krieger

Gotham Books

30 N Gould St.
Ste. 20820, Sheridan, WY 82801
https://gothambooksinc.com/

Phone: 1 (307) 464-7800

© 2023 C.J. Krieger. All rights reserved.

No part of this book may be reproduced, stored in a retrieval system, or transmitted by any means without the written permission of the author.

Published by Gotham Books (May 23, 2023)

ISBN: 979-8-88775-252-5 (sc)
ISBN: 979-8-88775-253-2 (e)

Because of the dynamic nature of the Internet, any web addresses or links contained in this book may have changed since publication and may no longer be valid.

The views expressed in this work are solely those of the author and do not necessarily reflect the views of the publisher, and the publisher hereby disclaims any responsibility for them.

TABLE OF CONTENTS

Introduction 17
A Word From The Author 18
Books by C. J. Krieger 19

POEMS

Soon Grandma 21
When Old Dancers Die 22
The Old Man Danced 24
The Rains 25
I Love You Too 26
What My Mother Looked Like 28
The Four Seasons 1978 30
    SUMMER 30
    AUTUMN 31
    WINTER 32
    SPRING 32
The four seasons 1992 33
    WINTER 33
    SPRING 34
    SUMMER 35
    AUTUMN 35
The Four Seasons 2017 37
    SUMMER 37
    AUTUMN 38
    WINTER 39
    SPRING 41
The Four Seasons 1987 42
    SPRING 42
    AUTUMN 43

    SUMMER 44
    WINTER 45
The Four Seasons 2006 46
    SPRING 46
    SUMMER 47
    AUTUMN 48
    WINTER 50
The Four Seasons 1998 52
    SPRING 52
    SUMMER 53
    AUTUMN 54
    WINTER 56
The Four Seasons 1983 57
    WINTER 57
    SPRING 58
    SUMMER 59
    AUTUMN 60
Your Smile Enchants Me 61
Dancing And Demons 61
When The Earth Turned Again 62
Six Miles Away 63
Tonight The Night Was Long 64
Sandra's Pen 65
Camp Fires & Love 66
Miles Away 66
Under A Crumpled Blanket 67
Gabby 67
Men Don't Cry 68
The Unveiling 68
Like Him 69
A Little Incentive 69
Walking Backwards 70
Into a Time Gone By 71
That Walk 72

A Normal Day	74
There's Christmas in Your Eyes	77
Constantinople	78
Portrait of a Woman Walking	79
I Remember	80
A Testament Of Hope	81
Absolutely Perfect	83
Time	84
Laughing Eyes	85
Tack In The Box	87
A Cold Road Home	87
Easter Dress	88
A Morning Of Perfection	89
A Fork In The Road	89
Long, Long Ago	90
A Blind Date	91
This Old Man, He Had One	92
She Dreams of Days to Come	94
Ours To Share	95
Togetherness	96
When We Were Once Young	98
A Flashlight For Julia	99
The Eyes Of The Beholders	100
Winter Words	101
Even Though	102
I Was Once A Child	103
First and Last	104
Each And Every Day	106
Point of View	109
Morning Light	110
A Time Gone By	111
Long, Long Ago	112
In The Dark	113

Afraid To Do Right	114
Only Human	115
Farmer Jane	116
Lying Eyes	117
Laughing Eyes	118
A Cold Road Home	120
The Dance of Laughter	121
Togetherness	122
It's Only The Wind	123
As The World Shifts Again	124
When Bison Run Wild	126
He Died	127
There's Always August	129
Unopened Tears	130
Ghosts	131
After The Storm	132
Trying To Push A Buffalo Home	134
A Morning Of Reflected Light	135
Autumn In The Air	136
A Winter's Field	137
This Really Is My Very Last Poem	137
Something Stupid Like Hello	138
Because She's Much Too Beautiful	139
A Time	140
Zen Buddhist Bird	141
Chance Meeting	142
Casabay	142
Firefly Train	143
Breakfast Breasts	144
Watching The River Run	145
The Lion Doesn't Sleep	146
A Song Of Frozen Birds	147
Where Sadness Goes	148

Morning Love	149
Fat Bamboo	150
How He Was Saved From The Demons	151
Beautiful	152
Screaming In Silence	153
Glasses	154
She Waits For Spring	154
Harlequin Lament	155
Sandra's calling	155
Death By Verb	155
Flowers In The Snow	156
August	157
Truth	158
Cocoa	158
I Saw The Night Mysterious	159
Bikini Waxed Smile	159
Abracadabra	160
When All My Poems Are Gone	160
A Photo	161
Where I Am Going	161
The HMS Jack McKay	162
A First Time Meeting	164
Until All The Leaves Fall Again	165
Patty's Underpants	166
Moving Meditation	166
Walls	167
A Cold Night Of Perfection	167
The Perfect Woman	167
Fundamentals Of A Busted Relationship	168
The Perfect Day	168
What To Do When It Rains	168
Like Him	169
Watching The River Run	169

Across An Empty Field	170
When She Was Gone	171
The Child Within	172
The Truth Of Lies	173
Morning Of Reflected Light	173
God Can Tell	175
The Obituary Of John Page	176
Nothing Left To See	176
Days Of Youth And Fish	177
Dreams Of Mary Anne	178
Bright Eyes	178
Dreams Of The Immigrant	179
It's A Miracle	180
Hobo's Story	180
The Scent Of Winter	181
Looking For Someone Like Me	182
Morning Of One	183
Merry Christmas	184
There's Christmas in Your Eyes	185
In The Mind of the Beholder	186
Alone in the Dark	186
She Knew, She Knew, She Knew	187
To Share It All With You	188
Alone in the Dark	189
The Color Of Picasso	189
Almost a Very Good Year	190
Camel Cigarettes	191
When The Leaves Fall	192
A Naked House	193
Passing Into Spring	194
The Truth Has Not Set Me Free	195
She Dreams of Days to Come	196
Constantinople	197

Never to be Heard From Again	198
Fireflies	199
1:43 In The Morning	200
He Still Whispers	201
Tomorrows	201
Like A Whisper In The Wind	202
Fallen Dreams	203
Arctic Dreams	204
Everyone Goes Away	205
What She Was Like	206
The Shadows of Tinker Street	206
A Gift Of Circles	208
What Coffee Can Never Replace	209
Is There A Soul?	210
Without Regrets	211
Fallen Dreams	212
Where Dreams And Rivers Flow	213
Tomorrow Today	213
Even Eagles Fall	214
When All My Words Have Run Away	215
Heaven's Gate	216
It's True	216
My Love	217
Things Change	218
I Can No Longer Understand	219
It's Raining Dreams	220
Gabby	221
Blackout	221
Angels Fly With Dragons Wings	222
Faces	223
Fingered Wings	223
Groups minus One	224
Snow Drops	225

She's Gone 226
Men Don't Cry 227
The Touch Of Love... 228
Richard Brautigan 229
The World's Fastest Cat 229
Buddha Based Soup 230
Lamplight Storm... 230
Origami 231
She Waits For Spring 231
Suddenly Beautiful 232
Those Magic Times.. 233
A Testament Of Hope 234
Bedroom Winter.. 235
Amalgamate... 236
What the Sea Has Taken 237
In Lieu of Passion 238
In the Quiet of Winter's Silence 239
A Paper Calls 241
Conflicted! 243
A Poem Of Frozen Birds... 244
An Agreement of Love 245
When It All Comes Together 245
Deer Prints In The Snow... 246
Paying Attention 246
Beneath Streetlights 247
Pieces Of Themselves.. 248
I Saw The Night Mysterious 249
Faucet Eyes.. 249
One Of The Best 250
Tears... 250
Pieces Of November 251
Almost Good News... 252
The Thievery Of Clouds 252

Two Quarts Down 253
Sometimes You Have To Sing.. 254
Absorbed By The Sun 255
Woodstock Mornings 255
The Lively Image 256
When Water Cracks 257
In The Third Person 258
I Have Never Not Seen 258
Changing Gears... 259
Bungee Jumping.. 259
Making Sense 260
Puss In Boots... 260
Youth As I Recall 261
In The Eyes Of The Young... 261
Snow Cat... 262
My Grandfather's Eyes 263

TO ALL MY DEAR AND WONDERFUL FRIENDS AND MOST ESPECIALLY

MIMI TURQUE

~~~~~~~~~~~~~~~~~~~~~~~~

For those of you who have not yet tasted his unique penning... take a moment to savour the way CJ takes us through the panoramic terrain he has called home. Feel the crisp wind as it travails the mountains... and the mists that clear to reveal the stunning beauty of each unique season.

Many times, I find his penning reaches in deeply, not only with his metaphors surrounding a stirring vista but also due to his astute, often tender, or witty insight into humanity. I hope you will also experience CJ's poignant works as profoundly moving... I'm sure you will!

Robyn Selters, Poet,
Blackall Range,
Queensland,
Australia,
4560.

~ ~ ~

Robyn and I are very much part
of a mutual admiration society.

I have been following Robyn's poetry for years. She is without a doubt, Amazing! You can find many of her wonderful poems on

https://allpoetry.com/robynselters

I believe, if you take the time to read just one of her many poems on that site, you will, (like me), find it difficult to just stop at one.

INTRODUCTION

Giving nature animation, his words are gentle, like his ageless soul, as we live in a time when people are more engaged in their blue screens than they are with blue skies, golden brown leaves, a glowing sun, and the love of another person.

C. J. Krieger reminisces and mourns over lost love, while he smiles and laughs over beautiful memories. We laugh and cry with him if we are old or wise enough to understand how time and the changes it brings affects our lives.

I have known Cecil [I call him "Ceej" for C.J. and I also call him "brother" because we are brothers in spirit] since Seventh Grade at Montauk Junior High School, in Brooklyn, New York. We became fast friends and remain so forever. So you probably think that I would be biased in my assessment of his poetry and you would be correct.

But knowing Ceej and reading his work puts me in a special category not only as a friend but as someone who feels what he feels when he expresses it. And the way he expresses it is from genuine experience that is so clear to me, that I can hear his voice speaking the words he has put to paper.

So, dear Reader, read his poetry and inhale his thoughts and emotions in each word. While you may see a snowfall, Ceej sees snowflakes dancing as he has danced so long ago.

Robert Hoey

A WORD FROM THE AUTHOR

Here I sit, five days away from the ripe old age of 76, and with each passing day, hour, minute and second that goes by I find myself less like taking the time to write. I think this is nature's way of telling me to take a break and do something different for a while.

With the road ahead of me, much shorter than the road behind, I have tried resetting my priorities. Certain things which I had put away, like music and going out for a walk on a beautiful day, or taking a ride in the country, I am pushing myself to do once again. And although it isn't easy to force myself to do these things, I try, nonetheless.

These days I also look for that special someone with whom I can share these later times of my life. My requirements have changed quite a bit from all those perfect features I wanted so long ago in my youth. These days she needn't be beautiful or trim but be happy, and a companion I can make smile who can do the same for me.

Well… that's it! So please feel free to dive in and enjoy my poetic thoughts. And if you find something that tickles your funny bone, or brings a tear to your eye, or a song to your heart, please… by all means, share it with anyone you like… even me!

C. J. Krieger

BOOKS BY C. J. KRIEGER

POETRY

Pinacolada Child
There's Always August
Absorbed By The Sun
Reflections In Glass
On Tinker Street
Leaving Woodstock By Walking Backwards
Before I Die, I Will Dance

~~~

WEBSITE

http://cjkriege2.wix.com/cjkrieger

~~~

'Love, Life & Dancing'
edited by
Robyn M. Selters

SOON GRANDMA

She has become
Like a thin Chinese teacup
Placed upon a large rock
She has become… fragile
Afraid to go anywhere
Least she break

She sits outside
When the weather is clear
Reading the same book
She has read for many years
Painfully turning the pages
With crooked fingers

Occasionally
I see her smile
As the lines on her face
Seem to multiply ten-fold
While she tries to remember
Why she is smiling

When the cooler weather
Dances around her
She wears a long soft scarf
Wrapped many times
Around her neck
To keep the cold away

Sometimes
She will ask me
"When will my friends
Be coming by?"
And I sit next to her
And hold her hand
Saying to her
Soon Grandma… soon

WHEN OLD DANCERS DIE

She was a dancer
But now at age sixty-seven
During the day
Her ghost leads small groups
Of aging seniors
In pilates stretching
Several times a week

She was a dancer
And though her feet
Remembers every heel and toe
That she had ever done
Arthritis keeps her
From ever thinking
Of a simple lock-step
Ever again

She was a dancer
Whose feet flew
This way and that
Across every stage
From New York to California
But was never chosen
To be the one
To play that special role

And though
She is sixty-seven
And the direction of time
Can never flow back
Somewhere
After the sun departs
And nighttime covers the land
She closes her eyes
And still dreams
Of the time

She was a dancer

THE OLD MAN DANCED

When times were hard
And life weighed down heavily
Upon his shoulders
The old man danced

When the true love
That was his forever
Left without rhyme or reason
To free himself from sorrow
The old man danced

When many years had passed
And love was replaced by loneliness
And all those he had cared for
Passed on into the ages
The old man danced

These days
Even though
He is much younger than he was
So, so many years ago
He never lets a day go by
Or lets a good deed go unsung
Unless he dances

And as time eventually frees
All the souls it touched at birth
And the brightness of life
Passes on into night

In the darkness there waits a soul
Who wants nothing more
Than to come into the light
And dance

THE RAINS

The rain washed down the mountain
Softening the warm earth
As I sat by my cabin window
Watching the muddy waters
Rolling down into the river below

The showers started five days ago
And from the first drop that fell
The rain continued to pour on and on
While the animals hid in their shelters
And I danced, soaking wet, beneath the clouds

It was the dance of a very young man
Filled with the folly of my youth
In the heat of a warm summer's day
Thinking thoughts that only come
To one so young and carefree

Looking back to that day
Which I remember as if it were just now
I can't help but smile
For it was a time of gaiety and merriment
That only one so young could know

Today I sit by my window
Watching the rain pound upon the land
Studying the muddy waters
As they roll down into the river below
Remembering that time gone by

And in the warmth of a summer's day
I threw open my front door
And as best as an old man could
I walked out into the summer's rain
And danced

I LOVE YOU TOO

When I am gone
Who will read my words to you?
All the poems about you
That I have put to paper
Will surely crinkle into dust
And slowly fade away
With every passing day

There are times
When I sit quietly
Reading all these wonderful stories
I have written about you
Bringing tears to my eyes
With the pain of missing you
More than I thought possible

But those were days
Of youth and clouds
And young unfilled dreams
That were dreamt by an old man
Who can no longer remember your face
Yet somewhere within my memory
I know you are there

I know because of the times
I wake in the early morning hours
And hear you say to me
I love you
Before the dream fades away
And I hear my voice calling back
Just before you are forever gone
I love you too

WHAT MY MOTHER LOOKED LIKE

I can't remember
What my mother looked like
That was so long ago
In a time of chasing butterflies
And childhood friends
Whose faces I can still see
When I close my eyes

I can't remember
What my mother looked like
But I can still recall
My dog Rex
As he jumped around me
When we played together
On the steps of my house

I can't remember
What my mother looked like
But I do remember my sister
With her beautiful smile
And loving way she helped me
Get through my younger days

I can't remember
What my mother looked like
But I do remember
My father's anger
And how his hands
Fell hard upon me
When he felt I needed it

I can't remember
What my mother looked like
But I can remember
How unmoved I was
When I heard my father died
I felt almost... relieved

There are many things
I can remember
And many things
I have chosen to forget
But after seventy-five years
Of life upon this earth
I still can't remember
What my mother looked like

THE FOUR SEASONS 1978

SUMMER

The old motor struggled
Against a non-existent breeze
As the overhead fan cut through the lifeless air
Trying desperately
To cool the slight figure
Lying quietly on the bed

The heat of the summer's day
Seemed to linger
While the darkness of night
Brought no relief
From the warm and humid air
Nestled in the room

Every so often summer is like that
As the hot muggy air
Tends to pull dreams far, far away
Dreams… that otherwise offer escape
Dreams that can take us
To thoughts of cooler times

AUTUMN

Autumn had come again
As I stood by my window
Watching the birds change color
And fall softly to the ground

In the distance
Flocks of leaves gathered
Upon the branches of the trees
Readying themselves
For the long flight south

I sipped on my cigar
And lit up a cup of coffee
Watching the smoke
Drift out my screen window

Yes
It was a day just like any other
Except autumn was in the air

WINTER

Out in a winter's field
My camera takes photos
Of white-tailed deer
Running about

Clicking…
As one by one
They run off into the woods

Until…
Out in a winter's field
My camera takes photos
Of an empty winter's field

SPRING

Spring has come on a fool's errand
Someone had told it, it was time
Time to wake the flowers
Time to chase away the morning's frost
Time to turn a young man's fancy

Who would have guessed
That lurking
Somewhere behind the cold Catskill Mountains
Old man winter sat snickering
At the foolishness of a retreating spring

THE FOUR SEASONS 1992

WINTER

In the middle of winter
I feel a summer madness upon me
A warmth
That radiates from your smile
Chasing the chill of the morning
Far, far into the sun

In the middle of winter
The heat of your thighs
Embraces me
Enfolds me
Until all the icicles
That once hung long
From the eves of my heart
Have forever gone

In the middle of winter
Even though the cold
Has taken the land
And enters all my dreams
When you approach me
My temperature rises
Until all that is left
In the middle of winter
Is summer

SPRING

Spring was dry
As I watched
The shattered leaves
Of last summer
Blow wildly about

The sun's bright rays
Dancing through the forest
Lit up the sky
Casting long twisted shadows
Far down
The old country road

I loved the smell
Of the spring flowers
Along with splashes of colors
Rising from the ground
It seemed to make the forest
Come alive

Yes
It was a good Spring day
As I walked down
The old country road
That led from my front door
Around the mountain
To that special place
That I loved to be

Absolutely… nowhere!

SUMMER

No blankets
Or sheets
Or coverings of any kind
Nothing but skin

On this warm summer night
As the gentlest of breezes flow
Dancing the curtains
Softly about

Outside the window
A star-filled night
Graces the heavens in a splendor
That seems paled beside her

How lucky and blessed
I am at this moment
To be walking by
With a camera in my hand

AUTUMN

I remember
It was the year
The grizzlies ran wild
And the snow fell
Before Autumn
Had a chance to fill the land

I remember
The cold nights
Filled with a new north wind
That pulled all the dying leaves
From the summer trees
Sweeping all the colors away
Leaving the forests bare
Except for a kaleidoscope of leaves
Whose patterns changed
As the wind whipped the forest floor

I remember
It was the year I awoke
And when I called your name
It returned to me
Echoing throughout the house
Without a trace of warmth
Only to fall
Soundlessly
In the emptiness
That you had left for me

This was an Autumn I remember
That I wished
I could not remember
At all

THE FOUR SEASONS 2017

SUMMER

It was one of the warmer summer days
Not a breeze or cloud in the sky
The humidity so high
I could almost reach out
And pluck it from the air

I watched the sunlight
Hitting the north side of my house
Seeking shelter then slowly roll away
Towards whatever little shade remained
With the speed of Grandma's Black Molasses

A few miles east of the old country trail
The river's waters had fallen
Lower than I had seen in years
Even the riverbanks had dried
Into a crumbling hard brown clay
That yearned for the rains to come

The heat, so oppressive and unyielding
Muted the voices of the birds
While all the wild animals
That usually ran about the fields
Sought out some relief or at the very least
Waited until night fell
Before coming out to play

These were the quiet days
The silent times of life
It was the summer of waiting
A time that I could no longer dance
Or sing, or see you under the starry sky
This was the summer you had gone
And I had grown much, much too old
To wait for another winter to come

AUTUMN

Autumn arrived
With a cool morning wind
And the rustling
Of golden brown leaves
That changed color
As they hysterically danced
Through the town streets
Before heading out
To their winter home

Here and there
Gangs of ferocious squirrels
Ran up and down the trees
Harvesting whatever fruits and nuts
That refused to drop
From the shivering trees
Whose bare bark
Could be heard
All about the woods

As I watched
Their once small mouths
Now bulging
With bits and pieces
Of summer's leftover bounty
Hurrying down
The old woodland paths
I couldn't help but smile

This is the time of year
That I enjoy the most
A time of transition
When the earth
Prepares for a long winter's nap
Yes, it most definitely was
(As I thought to myself smiling)
A time of scurrying squirrels

WINTER

Night inched its way
Up the north-east side
Of my house
Much in the way
A little child
Would climb over a fence
One small hand at a time

And as night's shadow
Reached the very top
It stopped for a moment
Before tumbling over

And falling down
The south-west wall
Plunging the house into darkness

It was a familiar winter night
But what I remember most
Was how much colder it seemed
Then other winters before
Nonetheless
Warm or cold
It was winter
Complete in every way
With winds like icy fingers
And falling snow
That seemed to go on and on
Forever

It was on a night like this
That I thought of you
A night
When I was overwhelmed
By everything that winter was
Compounded by a darker darkness
Than any nights I could remember
That had come before

And try as I might
I could not summon the sun
Or make it rise more swiftly
To free my mind
From unwanted thoughts
Nor could I find any solace
In the quiet, quiet
Of winter's silence

SPRING

The windows rattled
As the spring winds blew
Down from the mountains
And across the forest
As I watched the newly budded trees
Bend and sway

Although spring was here
It was a cold wind
That chilled my cheeks
As I pulled the hood
Tighter over my face

Walking home I watched
While last year's winter leaves
Scurried across the ground
Every so often stopping to rest
Before running out of view

I enjoy days like this
It keeps my thoughts from rambling

On thoughts of you
With your Easter dress and bonnet
Walking, walking, walking down
This old country path
Waving to me
For the last time

THE FOUR SEASONS 1987

SPRING

As I drove down the mountain
Fog covered the road
Like patches of thick cotton
While the sun
Starting to do its work
Cleared off portions of the Catskills
In varying bits and pieces

The ascending fog
Climbing high into the sky
Almost looked like rising smoke signals
With some grandiose dream
Of one day becoming a cloud

The morning lingered
And as I watched
The forest slowly and meticulously
Began to appear
Bits and pieces of the distant mountains
Gently emerged to find their places up ahead

It was just another spring morning
Right after the rains
And like a well-rehearsed magician
With a wave of his bright, light-filled hand
The sun made everything once hidden
Come leisurely into view

AUTUMN

Like soldiers lined up
With arms outstretched
And palms facing towards heaven
The barren trees lined the road
In a naked display

Leaves that once filled the landscape
Were now gobbled up
By autumn's frosty winds
Which seemed to have come and gone
Much more quickly
Than any autumn he ever remembered

Thinking back he realized
How hard he had tried to hold
On to each passing moment

Walking up this old country road
He knew it was time to let go
Time to stop looking back

For the very first time
In more years than he could recall
With the biting cold against his face
A shivering figure could be seen
Looking all around
At the beauty of autumn

SUMMER

The old motor struggled
Against a none existent breeze
As the overhead fan cut through the lifeless air
Trying desperately
To cool the slight figure
Lying quietly on the bed

The heat of the summer's day
Seemed to linger
While the darkness of night
Brought no relief
From the warm and humid air
Nestled in the room

Every so often summer is like that
As the hot muggy air
Tends to pull dreams far, far away
Dreams… that otherwise offer escape
Dreams that can take us
To thoughts of cooler times

WINTER

Tomorrow turned out to be yesterday
All over again
The only thing that was different
At least as far as I could tell
Was the date

The weather was lousy
And the phone still hadn't rung
As a matter of fact
No one had called for over three weeks
Bringing the question to mind
Why the hell do I need a phone!

Living out in the country had its advantages
The beauty of the land
The quiet of the countryside
The sweet smell of flowers in spring
Or the odor of hardwood burning in winter

I had decided long ago to live out here
In the beauty of nature
It gave me a chance to write
And to share my words with others

So here I sit
With words
Pouring from the tips of my finger
In paragraphs of dreams
And sentences of imagination
Hoping someday you might read this
And one day knock on my front door
And find me

THE FOUR SEASONS 2006

SPRING

The sweet smell of spring
Danced on the autumn winds
Under the eaves of the wooden cottage
Past the old rusted screens
Filling the room with fragrance
From the flowers that hid from view

Out past the garden
And far beyond
Into the dense green forest
That guarded the old house
From the music of fierce songbirds
That sang in the morning sun
She dreams of days to come

Though he cannot see her
Or hear the laughter
That comes when she thinks of him
Nor does he know that today
She wears her summer blue dress
Because he loved the way it fell
Across the curves of her body

Today the day will be brighter
The sky will be bluer
And the earth will turn more gently
Because she knows he thinks of her
Thinking of him
And like her, he dreams
Of days to come

SUMMER

My air conditioner groans
In the noon-day summer's heat
While unseen… except to me
I watch spring running about
Seeking shelter
In the far shady left corner
Of my meagerly furnished living room

Occasionally
During the cooler nights
When the north wind blows
It has popped its head out
With fingers crossed
While dark eyes stare
At the bright moon and stars
And cloudless skies

Fearless
Except for the light of dawn
Or a power failure
Or air conditioner malfunction

Hopeful
That summer won't last
And the cool autumn winds
Will blow
Into that far left corner
Of my meagerly furnished living room
Confident
That someday soon
Summer will pass
Into the much cooler days
Of autumn

AUTUMN

In the middle of autumn
We made love
On an old rickety bed
That clanked and squeaked
So very loud
That it made our neighbors
Who lived miles away
Smile

Even though
We are no longer together
Whenever I remember
Those wonderful times
There is nothing I can do
To stop a smile
From crossing my lips

But whenever that happens
There is a sadness that follows
A sadness that comes
With a question of why
Why are you no longer here?
Why, if we had such joy
Did I choose to be alone?

My memories of you
Are lonesome memories
Foolish memories
Memories of a young man
Who made the wrong decision
A decision
That can never be changed

A decision
That being alone
Was much, much better
Then having the love
Of a wonderful woman
Who shared an old rickety bed
That clanked and squeaked
So very loud
That it made our neighbors
Who lived miles away
Smile

WINTER

I stopped for a moment to listen
To the cold arctic winds
While they rolled down the mountain slopes
And as the sun withered in the morning sky
I went about getting my little cabin ready
For the coming of another winter

I watched the flowers in my garden
Shrivel softly into themselves
Before crumpling to the ground
Waiting for the end of autumn
And where they once had been
Whoosh... they were gone!

I was very sad to see all the colors
That once filled my garden
Fade to gray
But that was winter
Black and white
Including every shade of gray
Anyone could ever imagine

In preparation, I stoked the fires
Pulled my favorite chair
Up to the hearth
And with a book
Of my favorite poems "On Tinker Street"
I prepared for the coming
Of the cold, cold winter winds

Looking up to the sky
I could see flocks of birds
Reading themselves
For their long flight south
With the exception of one old Robin
Who called to me
From my window

Asking if he might come in
And stay warm
… It was winter

THE FOUR SEASONS 1998

SPRING

I can't take my eyes off of you
As you carry your beauty about
Much in the way
A spring sky carries the color blue

I watch outside my window
White cotton clouds
Slowly fade
Into the color of rain
Crying all of your beauty
Into a muddy painting
That washes through the town

As I watch the rain
Pouring down
I can't help but think
How beautiful
Are the tears of a warm rain
That dances upon my window
In spring

SUMMER

On hot summer days
When the ceiling fan
Slowly beats
Through the warm muggy air
She would sit
Outside the open window
Watching clouds
Roll quietly across the sky

Dreams of grown children
Would dance
In gardens long gone
And old dry rivers
Would run freely
Through her memories
As she watched the years
Through tears
Of younger times

On hot summer days
When the ceiling fan
Slowly beats
Through the warm muggy air
She would silently dwell
On days when she could run
And her mother
Would sit
Outside an open window
Watching clouds
Roll quietly across the sky

AUTUMN

When I was a child
The wind and I would play together
Tossing the autumn leaves on the ground
Dancing with the birds in the air
Making branches and flowers
Sway about like a ballerina
And whispering stories
That I shared
Only with my closest friend

When I was a boy
I no longer listened
To the words of the wind
Birds flew and colors changed
And the games we played
With all those we knew
Were more important than life itself
Because we were invincible

When I was a man
Autumns came and went
While I swept the autumn leaves
From the ground
Offering them up in a winter's pyre
And met my then
One true love
Who I knew would never leave me
And might someday be my wife

Now that I'm old
The seasons fly quickly by
While winter lingers on
Tonight I shall dance
With the birds of the air
And I shall watch branches and flowers
Sway like a ballerina with untold stories
Stories I can tell my children
And they to my children's children
So that they may know
Like them
I was once an autumn's child

WINTER

I remember the sound
Of a cricket chirping
As I sat by my winter window
Trying to decide
If I should call you
Or wait for you to call me

I remember how sad
The trees appeared to be
Hanging their heads in the falling snow
And as the sun peeked out
From behind the cold dark clouds
The melting snow drizzled
Into tiny streams of tears
That sought out the rivers
That sought out the sea

I remember your voice
Once so soft and gentle
Becoming quiet and still
While I searched for the words
That would say
How much I had missed you

I remember the first time
You didn't come home
Wondering how it was
I didn't see us growing apart
As I listened to a chirping cricket
Watching the falling rain with me
From my winter window

THE FOUR SEASONS 1983

WINTER

The ice fell from the clouds
Coating and bouncing off the highway

From time to time
The car shifted going down the road
As if the wheels had a mind of their own

Turning off the radio
To help concentrate on my driving
The hail sounded all about
Tic, tic, ticking with varying constant beats
All about and against the window
As the wipers frantically tried
To keep up with the cold frozen rain

The lights
Searching down the icy highway
Sparkled off the falling hail
Giving them the appearance
Of dancing diamonds

This was winter's last hoorah
A final stab at keeping spring at bay
A failed charge
Like the light brigade

While I
Was mesmerized
Steering down this gem-infested highway
With a front-row seat
To the beauty of driving through
The fall of winter

SPRING

She opened the curtain
In a darkened room
And the sun like water came rushing in
With light so blinding
That the flowers hanging in the window
Closed their eyes

On the rug, a shadow
Of a cat's tail tossing back and forth
She watched
As the old cat pondered it for a while
Then chased it into darkness

Steam from a hot cup of coffee
And smoke from a newly lit cigarette
Floated slowly out the window
Passing through a worn-out screen
Into the freshly washed spring air

With thoughts of gratitude
And a pair of worn-out jeans
She walked outside
With her floppy sun hat on
To tend her children in the garden

SUMMER

Surrounded by gold
As far as the eye can see
Above and below
It's summer again in the countryside

Children running about
Ripping flowers from the earth
In exchange for laughter
Scamper and hide along the lake
I often sit watching their small feet
Scurrying along the old winding paths
Kicking high into the air
The leaves of yesterday's fall

Bringing back to mind
My world as a child
Filled with summer warmth and magic
From two feet above the ground

AUTUMN

While my house slept silently
I stepped from the doorway
Into a cold October night
With the sweetening scent of autumn
And fresh fragrance of dying leaves
Dancing all about me

The wind guided me to that special place
A place where you and I always met
Only to find nothing
But a scattering of summer
Tossed haphazardly on the ground

I know that you have gone home
Back to the city lights and sounds of traffic
But next year
When we gather for summer
And the barn fires burn high
Touching the stars
I shall return here
To the sound of trees bursting with life
The stars falling into the morning
When the leaves of autumn come again

YOUR SMILE ENCHANTS ME

Your smile
Enchants me
Weaves in and out of me
Like my very breath

It is a spell
That you cast with nonchalance
Mesmerizing those about you
Man and woman alike

With an elegant wave
Of your leisurely arms
And a momentary glance
From your dark dreamlike eyes

I am lost
In your smile
That enchants me

DANCING AND DEMONS

She went out to dance
Saying that dancing
Shook off the demons
And made them fade
Far, far away

I woke up this morning
In Iceland

WHEN THE EARTH TURNED AGAIN

And the earth turned once again
As spring fell softly on the land
Between each raindrop that fell and dried
The sun brought rainbows of colors
That filled in the winter's snow

I watched as the cold gray clouds
Hastily ran north
Over mountains and fields
While the warmth of southern winds
Found places to build new nests
And the singing of birds
Replaced the winter storms

It was a year of fading youth
When childhood dreams
Could be remembered but not found
A time to put away childish things
And immerse myself in today

It was a time of old age
But not a time of sadness
A time to share
A time to receive
But most of all
A time when the earth turned once again

SIX MILES AWAY

The wind moved with a thunderous roar
Violently ringing the bells
On the east side of the house
Then suddenly quieting
As the winds changed
Now coming from the west

I watched as the night
Swiftly flew across the sky
And the moon occasionally
Peeked out here and there
Only to be hidden again by the clouds

I've always known where you lived
Just six miles down the road
A little off the beaten path
And though it's been three years
Since you had left
I have thought about those six miles

You have never called
Or answered my letters
And I have always looked for you
Around and about town

But your life has always gone north
And mine south
While you sleep
Somewhere down a beaten path
About six miles away

TONIGHT THE NIGHT WAS LONG

Night filled all the windows
While still a long way off
Morning was somewhere in the distance
Trying to find its way to my home

Occasionally I would glance outside
To see if there was a glimmer
Or a hint of light on the horizon
But tonight, the night was long

As I stretched out on my couch
Trying to fall back to sleep
You suddenly came to mind
Without rhyme or reason
I pictured you here beside me

I remembered you once told me
How you used to play piano
And somewhere in my need for sleep
And my struggle to think of you
I wished
I wished
I wished
I could hear you play

SANDRA'S PEN

In the cold of Vermont
I search
Up and down old Bianchi Street
Looking for you

Somewhere along the road
You have disappeared into your magic
By dipping your pen in words
And placing on paper
A poem from your heart

My sun is beginning to set
And Bianchi Street
Is growing colder and colder
But I now know how you survive
These cold Vermont winters
In your snow-covered home

It's in your pen
Filled with passion and stories
I can feel the heat
All the way down in Woodstock
Calling out
Saying
Read me, read me, please

CAMP FIRES & LOVE

The very first time
I looked into your eyes
And the whimsical way
That you smiled at me
While I watched you peeing
In the woods
I fell in love

MILES AWAY

They went into the shower
He closed his eyes
Seeing the warm water
Roll down the curves of her body
His hand tracing her softness
With thoughts of love
His excitement rising
Waiting for the moment
When both would be dry
And their hands would gently
Find the hidden secrets
Of the other
They went into the shower
With thoughts of the other
In homes miles away

UNDER A CRUMPLED BLANKET

I probed every corner
Touching where you'd been
Hoping to find your warmth
Liberated by the night
Searching for passion
Now hollow voids
Impressions left behind
Under a crumpled blanket

GABBY

Through a looking glass
With a quizzing gaze
She stares at me
Her camera eyes
And enchanting smile
Behind the reflection
Of a restaurant window
On a Woodstock road
To bacon and eggs

MEN DON'T CRY

It's like rain when I remember you
The sun could be shining brightly
Yet moisture seems to fall
And I don't know why
I am sure that no one sees me
I have places that I hide
I was told as a child that men don't cry
I try not to bother others
It would be a sign of weakness
Never say, suggest or otherwise imply
That my feelings overwhelm me
In the night when I sit lonely
You see, as a child I was told that men don't cry
Since I left you I have been drifting
Now it seems there's no salvation
I can't return or make these tears run dry
And the lessons of my childhood
Have lost their secret meaning
I don't understand the reason men don't cry

THE UNVEILING

I watch her legs
Unfurl
Like a tulip awakening
In the morning sun

Her lips
Soft and moist
Call out to me
With the fragrance of love

Is there anything
More exquisite
Than watching
A blossom unfold

LIKE HIM

His love for her was so deep
And so strong
That he would never allow her
To fall in love with a fool
Like him

A LITTLE INCENTIVE

At the airport
The colored ugly patterns
In the rugs
Were more than enough
To make anyone
Take the next plane

WALKING BACKWARDS

I have spent too many years
Walking backwards
Trying to retrace my steps
Looking for you
But every place I have gone
Has changed
It seems that nothing
Ever remains the same
And no one
Except for me
Remembers you

And though
They call me a fool
And tell me
That it's impossible
I still believe
That you are out there
Somewhere
Doing the very same thing
Walking backwards
Looking for me

INTO A TIME GONE BY

My days and nights
Fly like an eagle
On the wings of a broken wind
While high in the sky
A bright hot sun
Sheds a wintry light
On the little town
Of Woodstock

Up and down
Well-worn streets
Tired feet leave footprints
In the newly fallen snow
While winter shadows
Scuttle quickly down the road
Running
Running
Running into the darkness
Only to fade into the chill
Of a growing winter night

My days of summer
Have now gone
Long changed into spring
Then summer
And now into a final
Chilly winter
That has fallen upon me

As I stand here
In the center of Woodstock
I look behind
At my footprints
Now hiding in the shelter
Of my long, long shadow
A shadow that will soon
Vanish… into time

THAT WALK

I watched her
About a block or so away
Walking toward me
Her wheat blown hair
With silver strands
Tossed about
By a brisk northern wind
And that walk
A walk that only she knew
With a quick gait
Bouncing from side to side

I noticed her looking away
But knew her well enough
To know
She knew
That I was up ahead
And that she would suddenly turn
And with an act
Of total surprise say
Hello! I didn't see you there

We hugged
With a hug of old lovers
You know the kind
Sort of nice but restrained
And spoke of the lost times
Trying to fill the other in
As quickly as possible
On those unknown missing years
Knowing that soon
Each of us
Would be on our way again

So as the cold Canadian wind
Whipped all about
We told abbreviated stories
Of the passing years
Ending with a smile
Ending with a hug
Ending with a kiss
As I watched her
Turn and go on her way
With that walk
That walk that only she knew
You know the one
With a quick gait
Bouncing from side to side

A NORMAL DAY

The nurse left work
At five-o-clock
Followed by a midget
In a floppy-eared winter hat
Who looked something like
A small mixed breed dog
Caught between a Pit Bull Terrier
And a very old Mexican Chiwawa

This was the way it went
Every workday
For the last seven years
And unless you knew
That all of them worked together
At the county hospital
You would swear
That the circus was in town

It was an odd arrangement
As the management hired everyone
Sight unseen
According to their abilities
Not their appearance!

And in this small town
This particular hospital
Seemed to attract
An odd conglomeration of employees
From all four corners
Of the world

Returning home
To her small cold-water flat
She put up a pot of hot water
And as it heated
Decided on a cup
Of herbal lemon-grass tea
Before settling into
A very old lazy-boy chair

Reaching over to the table
She flicked the replay button
On her answering machine
And listened to all her messages
Or should I have said
All "one" of her messages

"Hi Mrs. Smith" (it went on)
"We have a problem
With the last check you sent
Could you"...
A loud click sounded
As she hit the erase button
And the tape ran backwards
Stopping with a thud at the end

It was the same message
She had been receiving
Every day (weekends too!)
For the last three months
Still, there was nothing to do
Work was sparse
And she was told over and over
How lucky she was
To still be working!

Totally exhausted
It only took several minutes
After turning the TV on
Before she fell off
Into a sound peaceful sleep
Only to be jarred awake
By the shrill sound
Of her alarm clock

A quick shower
A change of clothes
And a microwave breakfast later
With very little
On her mind
She was out the door
And walking to the hospital

It took about ten minutes
For her to arrive at the ER
Where she greeted the guard
With a sleepy morning hello
As I watched her walk in
Followed by a midget
In a floppy-eared winter hat
Who looked something like
A small mixed breed dog
Caught between a Pit Bull Terrier
And a very old Mexican Chiwawa

THERE'S CHRISTMAS IN YOUR EYES

I can see Christmas in your eyes
And jingle bells dropping from the trees
So loud
I cannot shout above them

If you cannot hear me
What does it matter if I say
I love you
My words are lost
In the ringing

In the sound
Of Christmas
In the sound of jingle bells
In the sound of quiet trees
Lost in the forest

CONSTANTINOPLE

Constantinople haunts my nights
In dreams both sad and stirring
Of wooden ships
Under star-filled skies
Searching for fortunes
Hidden by those long gone

As we sail away
Down the dark Euphrates
Shadowy eyes
Filled with lost dreams
Can be seen in the sadness
Of the forgotten
Waiting on the shrouded banks
Forever

Looking back
Toward the city lights
Reaching up
To the night sky
Constantinople waits
And waits
And waits
For me
And for you
To come

PORTRAIT OF A WOMAN WALKING

She has good eyes
Eyes that have not found winter
Quite yet
But eyes that long ago
Had left autumn
Far, far behind

Looking down empty streets
Filled with vacant benches
And bare trees
Whose leaves have long ago
Passed into yesterday
She walks about
Indifferent to the world

It's a time of change
A time of cold winds
And gray skies
Filled with meaningless clouds
That move this way
And then that

Skies
That just like her
Hold nothing but memories
And shadows of sunshine
That once filled lover's hearts
With possibilities of tomorrow
And unborn dreams

She has good eyes
Eyes that long ago
Once knew
Summer, spring and autumn
Eyes
That have not
Quite yet
Found winter

I REMEMBER

I remember
It was the year
The grizzlies ran wild
And the snow fell
Before autumn
Had a chance to fill the land

I remember
The cold nights
Filled with a northern wind
That pulled all the leaves
From the summer trees
Sweeping all the colors away
Leaving the forests bare
Like a picture
Taken in black and white

I remember
It was the year I awoke
And when I called your name
It returned to me
Echoing throughout the house
Without a trace of warmth
Only to fall
Soundlessly
In the emptiness
That you had left for me

I remember
That I wished
That I could not remember
At all

A TESTAMENT OF HOPE

Twisted and bent
My tired hands
With crooked fingers
Painfully write beautiful poems

My words have found a home
Here
On this paper you are holding
They have found a place to rest

Lately
My voice
No longer carries my words
Nor can it convey the passion
I had once felt

When I had written them

It's as though
They were placed here
Waiting for you
To raise them from the dead
And bring them back to life

These days
I have chosen my final road
With care
And though my end draws near
I see many blank papers
Waiting alongside the road
To record my journey

There will be no sorrow here
No tales of woe
Or love's lost stories

There will be no pity me's
Or hate to find along the way
Or even sadness
For deeds past done

Instead
I shall tell you of my dreams
Which until the final step
I still hope to fill
And of my love
That until the very end
I still hope to find

ABSOLUTELY PERFECT

If wishes were fishes
And baboons were bees

If smiling pink dolphins
Swam in polka-dot seas

If sunlight-filled cabinets
Sang all day long

And crickets and dragons
Played out on the lawn

Then all of the world
Would make perfect sense

'Cause horseshit and flowers
Would smell like incense

And I'd be insane
But you know that's not true

Well that's been my morning
Now let's talk about you!

TIME

At 7:12 am
The sound of footsteps
Were always the same
Neither heavy nor light
As they made a scuffing sound
Shuffling by the window
Along with the sound
Of a large dog's nails
Clicking on the ground

This particular morning
There were some new sounds
The sound of rain
Falling heavily on an open umbrella
And the splish-splash of feet
Walking down a wet street
A little more quickly than normal
Along with the sound of car tires
Splattering down a wet road
On the way to somewhere
Or maybe coming back
From someplace else

Checking the clock
He realized it was almost time
To get out of bed
And get ready for work
Besides
There was nothing else to hear
Because at 7:15

Everything seemed to quiet down
Until sometime after 12:27
Sometimes he wondered
If his friends were right
Maybe he was
Slightly obsessed with time
But at 8:38… who cares?

LAUGHING EYES

She didn't have to speak
All you had to do
Was look into her eyes
It was there
You could see the laughter
Or smiling or the tears
That never fell

And when she looked upon you
Her eyes held no secretes
They were honest eyes
That could
In the quickness of a breath
Tell you a story
From beginning to end

This winter
The nights go on forever
And in this rented room
Where I spend my time
This room
That grows smaller and smaller
With each passing day

I have grown to miss
Our quiet conversations
That we shared
When we looked upon each other

This winter
You are gone
And I have grown old
Yes... old
In this bare empty house

Sometimes in my loneliness
I forget myself
As though you are near
Feeling the warmth
Of your eyes upon me
And the laughter
That they shared
Echoing, echoing, echoing
Through the insanity of my mind
Until all that is left
Is the sound of
Your laughing eyes
Making me smile

TACK IN THE BOX

When he found out
She was deaf
He spoke louder
But then again
He wasn't the sharpest tack
In the box

A COLD ROAD HOME

The sun poured down like honey
Covering the land in a golden hue
But the angle of the sun
So very high in the sky
Kept everything it looked down upon
Cold and still

As he walked
He watched his breath
Spinning up in billows of clouds
Caught up in a twisting chilly wind
Only to be carried off
Before quickly fading away

No longer did he recognize
The quick step of his youth
Only a slow shuffling movement
On a road traveled too many times

Looking ahead
To his front door
He came to realize
With each shuffling step
That the nearer he drew
To his front door
The further away it became

EASTER DRESS

The windows rattled
As the spring winds blew
Down from the mountains
And across the forest
As I watched the newly budded trees
Bend and sway

Although spring was here
It was a cold wind
That chilled my cheeks
As I pulled the hood
Tighter over my face

Walking home I watched
While last year's winter leaves
Scurried across the ground
Every so often stopping to rest
Before running out of view

I enjoy days like this
It keeps my thoughts from rambling
On thoughts of you
With your Easter dress and bonnet

Walking, walking, walking down
This old country path
Waving to me
For the last time

A MORNING OF PERFECTION

Not a word was exchanged
In the early morning light
Just a cool wind
Blowing
Through the open window
Across the room
Over the bed
Cooling down the heat of passion
In the climax of a morning hello

As we looked at each other
She almost said… something

A FORK IN THE ROAD

I watch as you step into
The hot morning shower
While the water
Runs over your beautiful form

You are the earth
And the water
Are the roads
Of a Rand McNally map

Today
I shall go south
To where the road forks
And your summer's heat
Makes me yours

LONG, LONG AGO

She whispers promises
Spoken long, long ago
In soft quiet tones
Promises that have vanished
Like a morning fog

There remains nothing
Except echoes of stories
Told by townsfolk
Who still remember the music
And the dancing
Yes
The dancing
And smiling faces
Of those who came
Long, long ago

Woodstock still stands
But she no longer sings
With the voices she once knew
Gone too
Are the colored dresses and flowers
Of the ones who believed
That surely...
All this love can't die
It can't go away

But here
In this time
Many years later
All the dreams, hopes, and love
We once knew
Have become stories
On the lips
Of those who still remember
Long, long ago

A BLIND DATE

A sip and a question
A sip and an answer
Looking at each other
Trying to understand
Is this someone I want to know
Someone that might be good for me
A secret with the answers

And as time passes
We both try to decide
Watching the other
Fold and unfold their arms
Shoulders so high
That they are almost touching their ears

Listening carefully
As she fumbles for the right words
Knowing
That she just doesn't know how
To say
She's not interested

THIS OLD MAN, HE HAD ONE

The rain fell throughout the night
Pounding on every corner of the house
And though I could not see it fall
Through the blackness of the night
The sound echoed through the walls
Beating drum-like all about me

It was a hard night to sleep
As my body ached
And though I tried
I couldn't find a comfortable position
To stretch out
And let my dreams take flight

When I was young
I loved the rain
Watching at the window
While the drops rolled down
One into the other
Until they reached
The safety of the bottom

I still watch the rain
From time to time
I still watch the drops
Roll… one into the other

But there is no child here

He was left behind
A very long time ago
Hiding somewhere inside
Of this old man

SHE DREAMS OF DAYS TO COME

The sweet smell of spring
Danced on the autumn winds
Under the eaves of the wooden cottage
Past the old rusted screens
Filling the room with fragrance
From the flowers that hid from view

Out past the garden
And far beyond
Into the dense green forest
That guarded the old house
From the music of fierce songbirds
That sang in the morning sun
She dreams of days to come

Though he cannot see her
Or hear the laughter
That comes when she thinks of him
Nor does he know that today
She wears her summer blue dress
Because he loved the way it fell
Across the curves of her body

Today the day will be brighter
The sky will be bluer
And the earth will turn more gently
Because she knows he thinks of her
Thinking of him
And like her he dreams
Of days to come

OURS TO SHARE

When the cold north wind
Sweeps along
The icy rock hard ground
And the final remnants of autumn
Chill me
To the depth of my soul

I will remember
The love we knew
And the way your eyes
Smiled at the world around you

When the cold north wind
Comes knocking
On my door
I will not forget
All the love
You once had given me

A love
Ignited by a fire
That burned so very long
In a heart I once thought
Could never be warmed again

Though you have gone
From all I once held dear
Just the thought of you
Brings a warm glow
Deep inside

A warmth
That chases away
This cold north wind
Sending it far from the bed
Where we both had laid

A warmth
That not too far from today
Where autumn, winter
Spring and summer
All fall into the sun
And eternity is ours
To share

TOGETHERNESS

The headlights bounced
From the deer's eyes
Almost illuminating the road
Just before it turned
Running back into the forest

Tired
I slowed down
Pulling the old Ford
To the side of the country road
While I Closed my eyes
To rest for a few minutes

Leaning back in the driver's seat
I looked at the night sky
And a big old harvest moon
That danced through the stars

While my eyes fought my weariness
Memories of you
Came rushing in
As I felt my face relax
And a smile
Slowly cross my lips

Sometimes
When the moon is full
Casting shadows far into the night
I can hear the sound of you running
Through the forest
Over twigs and dry leaves

Right now
I can almost see
Your face peeking out
From behind a tree
Waving for me to come
As I watch you
Dance through the night
And then, dance away

WHEN WE WERE ONCE YOUNG

When the warm winter winds
Stayed north of the Dakotas
And blackbirds filled the sky
I would hear their voices
Bouncing off the Catskills
And across the old forest

It was a winter of cold sun
When the deep chilly snows
Could not cross the mountains
Keeping all the western storms
Far from the roads
That led to my front door

Sometimes
When the bison ran wild
Thundering across the open plains
I could hear their rumbling hoofs
Running down the twisting, turning roads
Into my dreams at night

This was a time of memories
A time of youthful imagination
Kept in that special place
That we call upon in later years
To remind us
Of the pictures we had painted
When we were once young

A FLASHLIGHT FOR JULIA

He pushes his love
Deep inside of her
Deep into a darkness
She wishes to share

Sometimes
He thinks of his penis
As a flashlight
Leaving no stone unturned

Yes...
He is on a mission
Searching, searching, searching
For that special place
That makes her
So... very, very... happy

THE EYES OF THE BEHOLDERS

Both were now
Sixty some odd years old
He
Wondered how someone who looked so young
Could feel so old

She
Wondered how all her friends
Seemed to appear
So much older
Than her

When walking down the street
Arm in arm
To any who could see them
They looked like
Crap

WINTER WORDS

She spoke to me
In winter words
Words she had filled
With ice and snow
Her words of summer
Have long since gone
The way of green fields
Covered in bright shining sun

There are days
Long ago
I can still recall
Her weaving a nest
With words of spring
Her love and warmth
Filled our home
With songs of warmth
And summer

But these days
She speaks
In winter words
Words
I should have
Long since seen
Before
Her winter words appeared
Her expressions
Spoke of autumn

EVEN THOUGH

Your photograph enchants me
You know
The one I took of you
So many years ago

I have looked at it
So many times
Over these passing years
That there is nothing about it
I do not know

And even though
I see your smiling face
Child-like grin
And soft brown eyes

Even though I can see
The way your skirt
Drapes carelessly
Over your knees

Even though I know everything
That there is to know
About this picture of you
Looking at me

A day never passes
Without me
Not wanting
To see it again

I WAS ONCE A CHILD

When I was a child
The wind and I would play together
Tossing about the leaves on the ground
Dancing with the birds in the air
Making branches and flowers
Sway about like a ballerina
And whispering stories
That I shared with my friends

When I was a boy
I no longer listened
To the words of the wind
Birds flew and colors changed
And the games we played
With all those we knew
Were more important than life itself
Because we were invincible

When I was a man
The autumns came and went
I swept the autumn leaves from the ground
Offering them up in a winter's pyre
And met my then
One true love
Who I knew would never leave me
And might someday be my wife

Now that I'm old
The springs, summers and autumns
Quickly fly by as winter lingers on
Tonight I shall dance with the birds of the air
And I shall watch branches and flowers
Sway like a ballerina with untold stories
Stories I can tell my children's children
So that they may know… like them… I was once a child

FIRST AND LAST

The old northeast wind
Came early
Rolling up the mountain
Towards the gray sky
While far off
Between the foothills
And the flowing river
A gathering herd
Of dark ominous clouds
Readied themselves
For the falling
Of the long winter's snow

It was the innocent year
A year when I was young
And the distances between us
Were much shorter
Back then my feet
Could swiftly cover the land

The forest ran wild
And how a long way off
Where the setting sun
Met the mountains
My sharp eyes could see
A heard of deer
Running about

It was the first year
My cat was in heat
Screaming throughout the night
Until I woke from my sleep
Went into the kitchen
And kicked her out of the house

It was the last year
I owned a cat!

EACH AND EVERY DAY

It was early morning
When the coffee started brewing
While down the hall
From the bedroom
Her words echoed
Past the old furniture
And tired old sleeping cat
Whose tiny black and white feet
Dangled off two thick phone books
Sitting next to the wall phone

Her voice
Seemed to annoy
All the old photos
Hanging on the wall
Causing a quick reaction
From the once smiling faces
As they all grimaced
In unison with a loud sigh
Before eventually
Reaching my ears

Turning my head
I watched for a while
At the quick darting tongue
Popping in and out
Of a Cheshire like face
And two adoring eyes
That seemed to follow me
While I walked about the room

Every time I stopped
To continue with my work

A deep grating meow
Followed by a short stillness
Echoed through the silence
Like a proper expected response

This seemed to be
The normal routine
In the early morning hours
Until a small figure of a woman
Shuffled into the kitchen
Poured a small amount of milk
Into her cup of waiting coffee
And with a long satisfying ahhhhh
Sat herself down at the kitchen table

On this particular day
Autumn seemed to have arrived
With a cool westerly wind
And the rustling
Of golden brown leaves
As they hysterically danced
Through the town streets
Before heading out
To their winter home

Here and there
Mobs of ferocious squirrels
Ran up and down trees
Harvesting whatever
They could find
That refused to drop
From the shivering trees
Whose bare bark matched
Gangs of local barking dogs
That ran about the town

Sipping on my coffee
I stared at the squirrels
Whose mouths now bulging
With bits and pieces
Of summer's leftover bounty
Ran hither, thither and yon
All about the streets

This was
My normal daily morning
Day in
Day out
For as far back
As I could remember

My normal routine
Done, without rhyme or reason
As is with any task
That is repeated
Each and every day

POINT OF VIEW

He didn't understand
What it was about carousels
That she loved so much?

But after thinking about it
For sometime
He came to the conclusion
What did it really matter anyway?

She didn't understand
What it was about her
That he loved so much?

MORNING LIGHT

Lying in bed
Her bare shoulder
Reflected the morning light
That fell lazily in from the window
While at the foot of the bed
A sheer cotton dress
Which had fallen in upon itself
Lay in a happily content pile
Without any ambition at all

On the opposite side of the bed
Lay a second pile
That seemed to have been
Thrown haphazardly about
In a determined effort to move
As quickly as possible
By removing themselves
From their owner
With only one single purpose

As sunrise filled the room
And dawn danced upon the roof
He found a peaceful place
To put all of his problems
And a place to rest his head

On a beautiful bare shoulder
That was filled
With nighttime memories
And reflected morning light

A TIME GONE BY

My days and nights
Fly like an eagle
On the wings of a broken wind
While high in the sky
A bright hot sun
Sheds a wintry light
On the little town
Of Woodstock

Up and down
Well-worn streets
Tired feet leave footprints
In the newly fallen snow
While winter shadows
Scuttle quickly down the road
Running
Running
Running into the darkness
Only to fade into the chill
Of a growing winter night

My days of summer
Have now gone
Long changed into spring
Then summer
And now into a final
Chilly winter
That has fallen upon me

As I stand here
In the center of Woodstock
I look behind
At my footprints
Now hiding in the shelter
Of my long, long shadow
A shadow that will soon
Vanish… into time

LONG, LONG AGO

She whispers promises
Spoken long, long ago
In soft quiet tones
Promises that have vanished
Like a morning fog

There remains nothing
Except echoes of stories
Told by townsfolk
Who still remember the music
And the dancing
Yes
The dancing
And smiling faces
Of those who came
Long, long ago

Woodstock still stands
But she no longer sings
With the voices she once knew
Gone too
Are the colored dresses and flowers
Of the ones who believed
That surely…
All this love can't die
It can't go away

But here
In this time
Many years later
All the dreams, hopes, and love
We once knew
Have become stories
On the lips
Of those who still remember
Long, long ago

IN THE DARK

We had grown
Further and further apart
Until reaching a place
Where she didn't even acknowledge
That I was in the same room

As she walked by my room
Unconsciously
She reached in
And turned off the lights

I said
I'm in here
So she apologized
Saying that she didn't see me
But that's how it was
She didn't see me any longer!

She stayed for a while
As we chit-chatted a bit
Trying to make up
For the mistake
And then went along her way

As she left
She turned off the light
And closed the door
Leaving me in the dark
Once more

AFRAID TO DO RIGHT

We are so much in love
That we are afraid
To make mistakes

So afraid that we might do
Something wrong
That we do nothing right

ONLY HUMAN

I love Jesus
And Jesus loves me
Although
There are times
When we each see things
A bit differently

Now I'm not saying
That he's always right
But then again
Neither am I

You see
After much thinking
And reading
And of course
From time to time
Talking things over with him
I have come to
The following conclusion

And that is
When it really gets down to it
Both of us
Are only human!

FARMER JANE

I watched her lie back
As my eyes followed the curves
Enjoying the symmetry
That was her left breast

She was a fertile field
That over the years
Had been well-kept
And of course well-plowed

And like the good farmer
That she was
She knew when it was time
To rotate the crops

And what time of year
To nourish the fields
In order to bring in
The richest harvest

As I moved about the room
As my eyes followed the curves
Enjoying the symmetry
That was her right breast

LYING EYES

Sometimes at night
Memories come rushing in
Tearing away reality's curtain
With recollections of days past gone

Staring at her from his chair
His eyes cut deeply
Peeling away the old skin
Of the elderly woman before him
Only to reveal the young girl
He had come to love

Though the years
Have buried her youthfulness
And time has taken its toll
His eyes could never see
How this girl changed
Into a tired old woman

A woman
Who just like him
Was so very happy
When they looked at each other
And their eyes
Lied

LAUGHING EYES

She didn't have to speak
All you had to do
Was look into her eyes
It was there
You could see the laughter
Or smiling or the tears
That never fell

And when she looked upon you
Her eyes held no secretes
They were honest eyes
That could
In the quickness of a breath
Tell you a story
From beginning to end

This winter
The nights go on forever
And in this rented room
Where I spend my time
This room
That grows smaller and smaller
With each passing day
I have grown to miss
Our quiet conversations
That we shared
When we looked upon each other

This winter
You are gone
And I have grown old
Yes... old
In this bare empty house

Sometimes in my loneliness
I forget myself
As though you are near
Feeling the warmth
Of your eyes upon me
And the laughter
That they shared
Echoing, echoing, echoing
Through the insanity of my mind
Until all that is left
Is the sound of
Your laughing eyes
Making me smile

A COLD ROAD HOME

The sun poured down like honey
Covering the land in a golden hue
But the angle of the sun
So very high in the sky
Kept everything it looked down upon
Cold and still

As he walked
He watched his breath
Spinning up in billows of clouds
Caught up in a twisting chilly wind
Only to be carried off
Before quickly fading away

No longer did he recognize
The quick step of his youth
Only a slow shuffling movement
On a road traveled too many times

Looking ahead
To his front door
He came to realize
With each shuffling step
That the nearer he drew
To his front door
The further away it became

THE DANCE OF LAUGHTER

Although you have been gone
These many years
Your shadow still remains
On everything
That you had touched

No matter where I go
There is no place
Where I cannot see
Or hear your voice
Filled with merriment and mirth
As it meanders
About the rooms

And though
You have departed
So many years ago
When my laughter
Pierces through the dark
I have found
The light of your smile
Still dancing on the laughter
That dances on my heart

TOGETHERNESS

The headlights bounced
From the deer's eyes
Almost illuminating the road
Just before it turned
Running back into the forest

Tired
I slowed down
Pulling the old Ford
To the side of the country road
While I Closed my eyes
To rest for a few minutes

Leaning back in the driver's seat
I looked at the night sky
And a big old harvest moon
That danced through the stars

While my eyes fought my weariness
Memories of you
Came rushing in
As I felt my face relax
And a smile
Slowly cross my lips

Sometimes
When the moon is full
Casting shadows far into the night
I can hear the sound of you running
Through the forest
Over twigs and dry leaves

Right now
I can almost see
Your face peeking out
From behind a tree
Waving for me to come
As I watch you
Dance through the night
And then, dance away

IT'S ONLY THE WIND

I watched
As the northern wind
Hollowed out the leaves of summer
Turning them to glass
Whisking them away
To winter skies

The frost on my window
Reminded me
Of simpler times
Far ago and long away
When I was a child
Who loved to play

But these days
I watch
As the leaves turn to glass
Fading into shivering clouds
Of children
Who dance in the snow

And though my hearing
Grows dim
There...
At my door
The northern wind
Waits for the summer
In me

AS THE WORLD SHIFTS AGAIN

The wind shifted
While the tree branches
Once bending east
Lifted, and then bent south
As a chilly north wind blew

The nights once warm
Now teeter-tottered on cold
Summer had ended
And the long fingers of fall
Dug deep into the earth
As the world shifted again

These days it is hard
Finding the right words
Even now as I write
This doesn't feel like a poem
More like the jabbering
Of a mad poet without direction

There were times
When words would flow
Like the waters rolling down
Barren rocks in high places
Only to find themselves
Trapped by my pen on paper

But still
The north wind blows
And the flowers that danced
In the warmth of the sun
Like me
Prepare to sleep
Until spring returns
And the world shifts again

WHEN BISON RUN WILD

Sometimes
When bison run wild
Across the open plains
Of my mind
I can hear
Their thundering hoofs rumbling
Down the twisting, turning roads
Of my dreams at night

Sometimes
When bison run wild
My memory fills
With herds of buffalo
On wide-open plains
Keeping alive
That special place
I had painted
When I was young

Sometimes
When bison run wild
I can almost hear
Their rumbling hoofs
Weaving and winding
Into my dreams at night
Waking me
In the early morning hours
With one hell of a migraine

HE DIED

In a war
That wasn't his own
He died

He now returns
Like the feet
Of a Flamenco dancer
Gliding over
A stained oak wood floor
Tapping out a beat
Taught to him
By those
Who have passed before

He went
Without question
To a war
That wasn't his own
And he died

Like a chess player
Who cannot prevail
But hopefully waits
For a mistake
So he might turn the tables
And win a game
That cannot be won

He returns
To his family
Who does not celebrate
His triumphs or victories
Because in a war
That wasn't his own
He died
He's dead
He's gone
He cannot return
And all the Flamenco dancers
And chess players in the world
Don't mean
A fucking thing

THERE'S ALWAYS AUGUST

It was late July
The day was charcoal gray
While the drizzle played
With the green moist grass
Bewildered raindrops fell
Ringing to the ground
She quietly sat
On the garden bench
Not wishing to go inside
For within the home
Hungry saddened memories
Stalked the halls
Her dreary mind
Would not allow her
To pass unnoticed
The only joy
Were the caged birds
Singing to be fed
It was late July
The sun had departed
Her damp wet clothes
Made her tremble
Keeping hope alive
She kept repeating
…There's always August

UNOPENED TEARS

I can see
That you have hidden them with guile
Placed them behind
A pasted-on smile
Somewhere down deep inside all the while
You've locked them away with a key
Hoping some day
They will set themselves free

I can see
Locked far deep inside
Within the far corners
Of both of your eyes
Between the bravados
And soft saddening sighs
In a place where you've driven your fears
Are lakes, and oceans and rivers
Of unopened tears

GHOSTS

They follow me
Some of them I know
Some of them I don't
But they follow just the same

At times
When the world is quiet
I hear them speaking
Always asking questions
Or telling me stories
I do not want to hear

Or late at night
Thump, thump, thump
They just have to
Walk about
As though I have
Nothing better to do
Then listen to them
Stomp around the house

Life is hard enough
Than having to deal
With "no life" at all!

AFTER THE STORM

The pounding rain
Beat
Like a toddler's hand
On an old Indian drum
Waking up memories
That I had long forgotten

Songs
That I knew so well
But have forgotten
Now decide to return
Chattering aimlessly on
About why
They decided
To come again
On this particular day
Which of course
Made me smile

Throughout the day
No matter how hard
I attempted to ignore it
The old music kept playing
In my head
So for the rest of the day
Though I tried
The music continued
To follow me
Everywhere I went
Growing louder and louder
Until my whole day

Was a medley
Of the 1960s

Note: My headache kept getting worse

It was just about this time
That a second cup of coffee
Would have been perfect
But the hurricane
That had just passed
Blew all the electricity
Away

Not being
A campfire kind of guy
Boiling water
Was not in my nature

After some time
I lit up a second cigarette
While drinking what remained
Of my cold
Once hot morning coffee
Half & Half without sugar

About this time
I was fairly certain
If I waited long enough
The single cup
Would work its magic
And chase my sleepiness away

So
I drank what remained
Closed my eyes

Leaned back
And fell fast asleep

It was typical

TRYING TO PUSH A BUFFALO HOME

She was no longer young
But not quite old
Still deep in her soul
She was a romantic
Believing in love at first sight
And of course
Soul mates
On starlit nights
She would go outside
Looking up at the sky
Repeating the poem
"Star light, star bright"
Making a wish
On the first star that appeared
In the end
When all the wishing was done
And dreams unfilled
She would walk into an empty home
With hopes of tomorrow
Sometimes she thought smiling
It was so difficult keeping the faith
Almost like
Trying to push a buffalo home

A MORNING OF REFLECTED LIGHT

This was a morning of reflected light
Off the teacups
Dangling from the cupboard hooks
While down the hall
Several voices in conversation could be heard
Around an old breakfast table
In a country kitchen

This was a morning of reflected light
That returned youthful memories
From when as a child
The smell of coffee and hot buttered toast
Seemed to permeate the air
Smells
That have since thinned through the years
Along with voices in the old tongues

This was a morning of reflected light
That played off the old read books
That lined the shelves
That covered the walls
That were no longer read

This was a morning of reflected light
That danced on five dusty guitars
And off the hands of an old musician
Who enjoyed the music
That was no longer played

This was a morning of reflected light
And for all its sadness
The memories it allowed
Made it a most wonderful morning

AUTUMN IN THE AIR

Autumn had come again
As I stood by my window
Watching the birds change color
And fall softly to the ground

In the distance
Flocks of leaves gathered
Upon the branches of the trees
Readying themselves
For the long flight south

I sipped on my cigar
And lit up a cup of coffee
Watching the smoke
Drift out my screen window

Yes
It was a day just like any other
Except autumn was in the air

A WINTER'S FIELD

Out in a winter's field
My camera takes photos
Of white-tailed deer
Running about

Clicking…
As one by one
They run off into the woods

Until…
Out in a winter's field
My camera takes photos
Of an empty winter's field

THIS REALLY IS MY VERY LAST POEM

When the night wind blows
And I quietly sit alone
While the television hums in the background
Words come to me

Sad words of longing
And poetry that speaks of tenderness
I want to remember happier times
Your smiling face filled with laughter
That echo from places
Now so far, far away

Especially the sound of your voice
That I have dearly loved
And committed to memory
A voice you now share with others

So with these words
In this ungodly morning hour
I write my last poem
To you

SOMETHING STUPID LIKE HELLO

From the corner of my eye
I watch her look at me
From the corner of her eye

I know she wants to turn
To look at me, and smile
But just like me, she is shy

So we both smile
In other directions
Hoping the other sees
And maybe says something stupid
Like… Hello

BECAUSE SHE'S MUCH TOO BEAUTIFUL

She never looks both ways
When she crosses the street
She's much too beautiful

And never has to wait for help
When she walks into a store
She's much too beautiful

She never worries about dates
There is always someone beside her
Because she's much too beautiful

But when she is alone
By herself
She wonders about love
True love

And if anyone can see
Beneath the surface
Beyond the beauty

Sometimes wanting
All that beauty
To go far, far away

A TIME

It was a time
Of frozen mornings
And barren trees
While I watched
The sky darken
As bit by bit
Pieces of the sun
Cracked
And fell away

It was a time
Of miracles
And changes
A time
When the earth
Once filled with green
Turned snowy white
Much like
The color of my hair

It was a time
When I was alone
In the night
And my thoughts
Filled empty rooms
With voices of those
I had loved
Dancing to
Lost music

It was a time
That I heard
From a distance
My voice repeating
Over and over
And over again
It was a time
It was a time
It was a time

ZEN BUDDHIST BIRD

A Buddhist bird flies
Under the eyes
Of winter's sun
As I watch his flight
Across a lonely wintry sky
Gazing up
At his long, long flight south

He diverts himself
From the chilly northern wind
A wind
That the sun cannot warm

He diverts himself
With a single thought
As only a Zen Buddhist bird might do
And asks

What is the sound
Of one wing flapping?

CHANCE MEETING

From across the supermarket
I saw an old lover of mine
Who I met
Several minutes later
In aisle three

Passing each other by
We both lied
As we said
Hello

CASABAY

The Casabay shoreline
Rolled way far down south
Where the crocodiles met with the sea
And the gulls fly about
Seeking salmon and trout
To serve with their crumpets and tea

Now the lanterns that lay
By the picnic parade
Where we all gathered and packed in a group
Waiting for lemmings
To jump from the cliffs
Into pots for our mixed lemming soup

Later that day
When the sun ran away
I watched
As the moon rose on high
We shook hands and hugged
While we drank our last mug
And bid bye as the day passed away
By the shoreline of old Casabay

FIREFLY TRAIN

The train had left
Less than a minute before I arrived
So I stood on the old platform
Watching it fade into the darkness

As the lights grew smaller and smaller
It gave the appearance
Of a cloud of fireflies
Evaporating into a cold winters night

Rounding the curve
The train lights slowly disappeared
One by one
And I couldn't help thinking to myself
That one of those fireflies was you

These days… as strange as it might seem
Whenever lazy fireflies flash in a warm summer's night
My mind sees pictures of you
Fading into winter on a firefly train

BREAKFAST BREASTS

Come sleep with me tonight
It's much too late to leave
All the taxis have gone home
The horses died so long ago
Moreover, the blanket was made for two
And this pillow knows your name
Besides, I love the way
Your perfect breasts look at breakfast

WATCHING THE RIVER RUN

I keep watching the river run
Always twisting
Always turning
It's there I sit
Beneath your eyes
And mull over dreams of paradise
With you
Someplace where the sky is white and blue
Yet I'm thinking much too much
And I hate walking alone
It's not often that I ponder such
But when I wander
Thoughts come rushing in
Willy-nilly
I don't have a special place
Where all these thoughts begin
From the left
And from the right
Without warning
They attack me when I wake
Early in the morning
I wish I knew what I had done
So I'll sit here
With you standing there beside me
Beneath your eyes
Beneath the skies
Where clouds and birds and angels fly
And listen to the waters running free
As you watch me
Watching the river run

THE LION DOESN'T SLEEP

His eyes
Dulled by years
Of iron bars and cold hard ground
Paces in circles
Looking but never seeing
Past the cage that holds his soul
First one way
Then another
Worn, torn and beaten by time
While those who come to look
And gaze at this king
Say
What a magnificent beast
What a beautiful animal
But all that really remains
Is a coat of skin
And sad shrouded eyes
Pacing day and night
In never-ending circles
First one way and then another

A SONG OF FROZEN BIRDS

It was an unexpected chill
As the icy north wind
Pierced like a shooting needle
Through the morning sun
So cold
That you could almost see it
Tumble down the mountainside

It was a morning of frozen birds
Falling like rain from the sky
Off the boughs of trees
Dripping down
And splashing like colored drops
On the rock hard ground

As I walked the wintry woods
I pictured the ice-cold wind as a brush
Painting the woods with drops of color
Bird colors of blues, greens and reds
That seemed to come alive
And sing

WHERE SADNESS GOES

I watched a tear
Appear in the corner of his eye
Fall into his beard
And disappear forever

So I sat
And wondered

Where does sadness go
When it falls into a beard

Is there some secret place
Hidden within the hairs
That sad tears hope to find

Now as for myself
I've been feeling kind of down
And the last thing I need
Is any more sadness in my life

So I made certain
Sadness could not find me
As later that night
I shaved off my beard

MORNING LOVE

And as the rains lightly danced
On the cold hard ground
The sun rose up quietly
On the background of a steel gray sky

With each raindrop that fell
I watched as the cracked earth
Became soft and smooth
With the beauty of mud

All this, while you and I
Fell helplessly into each other's arms
Rolling and tumbling to the beat
Of rain tapping on the windowpane

As we whispered our forever love
To the morning, to the rain
To the sun that hid in a steel gray sky
While we told each other the lies
We needed to hear

FAT BAMBOO

It felt funny just to say it
"Fat Bamboo"
Try to say it out loud
Doesn't it sound funny to you?
Almost as if the two words
Had no business being together

But what if there was such a thing
What could you do with fat bamboo?

I think I would build a house
A log cabin… a fat bamboo cabin
With floors made from fat bamboo boards
And a nice strong couch of fat bamboo

When the sun goes down
I will light up the house
With fat bamboo lamps
And watch the fat bamboo flames
Cast fat bamboo shadows
All about my fat bamboo walls

I would also make a fat bamboo bed
And when the night was right
I would take your hand and lead you
Into my fat bamboo bedroom
And make fat bamboo love to you

HOW HE WAS SAVED FROM THE DEMONS

So the mystic turned another card
He thought and then he said
There are eight demons in your heart
And one inside your head
The tired figure raised his brows
Then whispered more than spoke
Is there some way that you can help
Some chant you can invoke
Yes the mystic's voice replied
But such things are not cheap
For you see I'm old and frail
And this will drain me deep
But for a price this can be done
As he made a shaman's sign
That raised his strength to meet the task
And chased away the nine
The tired figures weight now gone
Raised lightly from his chair
And paid the mystic for his work
A price that was quite fair
Before you leave just one more thing
The sage's voice implied
I'm much too old to do this twice
And showed the man outside

BEAUTIFUL

Her head bowed and eyes down
In a dress so plain it fell into the wall
A woman of unapparent features sat
While all about her others were dancing
Still… nobody seemed to look her way
Halfway through the night with many gone
The music whispered two words to her
Come dance
The notes begging over and over
To leave her space of isolation
A calling that slowly became a feeling
That unexpectedly made her rise
With exquisite movements
Her body found itself in delicacy
Stopping all about her
Each eye hoping that someday
They might be as wonderful
And as she danced
She found herself
Suddenly
Beautiful

SCREAMING IN SILENCE

In the country sounds change
Thunder becomes a canon
Crickets are noisier than a diesel
And on the quiet nights
Silence grows so loud
That no other sounds
Can be heard above it

There were many who said
The two of them
Were made for each other
Still others who believed
That they had grown apart
If you never knew them
You would say
They were in love

So they lived together
In a mutual fabrication
Of visual adoration
While over the years
As conversation festered
And eventually faltered
They screamed at each other
In silence

GLASSES

We were together for 42 years
She was 64 **standing** in front of the mirror
Isn't my body like a 40-year-old she said
I was in a panic looking for her glasses

SHE WAITS FOR SPRING

On a snow-covered mound
Near a gray frozen river
At a table where there should be none
Winter's jacket is wrapped
About her frail figure
Measuring deeds she had done
Not feeling the cold or the sun
And waits for the river to run

HARLEQUIN LAMENT

Her dreams are found in Harlequin
In words so very far away
Her beauty hidden by a room
That sits just north **beside** the bay
On barren rock no lands abound
A lighthouse eye searches the sea
Escorting ships to harbors sound
She waits for love to set her free

SANDRA'S CALLING

Your voice
I know it
So very well
That even before
You call
I hear you say
Hello

DEATH BY VERB

She shot off her mouth
Just once too often
The last shot killed him
Right through the heart

FLOWERS IN THE SNOW

If flowers would grow in the snow
I'd live in winter's frozen hand
And run barefooted through the fields
Past frozen trees with icicle leaves

If flowers would grow in the snow
I know my heart could find a way
To shovel through the roads that lead
Past guarded gates back home to you

If only… flowers would grow in the snow

AUGUST

It was late July
The day was charcoal gray
While the drizzle played
With the green moist grass
Bewildered raindrops fell
Ringing to the ground

She quietly sat
On the garden bench
Not wishing to go inside
For within the home
Hungry saddened memories
Stalked the halls

Her dreary mind
Would not allow her
To pass unnoticed
The only joy
Were the caged birds
Singing to be fed

It was late July
The sun had departed
Her damp wet clothes
Made her tremble
Keeping hope alive
She kept repeating

… There's always August

TRUTH

It's not always about love
Watching her nakedness
Sprawled across the bed
Sometimes he said smiling
I just want to fuck your brains out

COCOA

The water slithered off the road
Like a snake seeking shelter from the sun
My clothes flooded with water
Clinging to my skin made a slow journey
The rain feeling more like flies
Pelted cold against my face
It was only a short distance
From my house to the store
A distance I normally covered quickly
Now seemed never-ending
The small store grew
As I closed the distance
And shortly loomed over me
Walking through the door
The water puddled on the floor
While I stood
Trying to remember why I came
Turning about I began once more
To walk back home
With one thought in mind... Hot cocoa

I SAW THE NIGHT MYSTERIOUS

Once when young
I saw the night mysterious
With moon and stars and lights in flight
It made me very curious
I thought the moon
So all alone
Amidst the stars that brightly shone
Reflected light that made me feel
Delirious
Until I realized
The feeling wasn't serious
But as I sit
I must admit
What lies ahead I can't predict
When daylight fades
And dark shades fall on us
I still can see the night mysterious

BIKINI WAXED SMILE

Hey you
With the smile of an angel
And your devilish intentions
Are you going to let me in
To your happy hunting ground
Or do you just plan
To make me look all night
At your beautiful
Bikini waxed smile

ABRACADABRA

She often gives herself
To others freely
Each time thinking
It will make her
More beautiful

WHEN ALL MY POEMS ARE GONE

When all my poems are gone
I shall dream
Of wordless rhymes on empty papers
Written by inkless pens

They shall flow
Endlessly and forever into the seas
For all to hear
On each breaking wave

And I shall sit on sandless beaches
And wait
And wait
And wait for my poems
To come in

A PHOTO

I only have one photo of her left
Out of the hundreds I had when I was younger
But still, I have a picture of her in my mind
I took a tack and put the last photo of her
On the wall
Hundreds of times
So the photo is filled with many holes
Although I can still see her in my mind
Sitting on the bay in Provincetown
Smiling at me
God I miss her
But these days all I have left
Is a photo of her
Filled with many holes
A photo that is slowly fading

WHERE I AM GOING

Show me a distance I haven't traveled
Show me a star I have never seen
Show me a land I've never walked on
And I'll show you the place I should be

THE HMS JACK MCKAY

On the banks of the Bond*
Down by a place called Lily-Pond
Stood a young man
By a Cat Napper Tree*

And his face though in stone
Is best described as grinning long
Due to a bottle
He had thrown in the sea

Now the words that he wrote
Were scribbled down in fountain pen
Lost with his ship,
He was left there to be

But the fates as they will
Cast this bottle on the shore
And so to the world
Came this message from he

I have long been alone
Thrown down upon this paradise
All that I might
Ever need's here for me

Still the touch of a hand
Is what I yearn for most of all
A small chance for love
And some sweet company

Now a tear left his eye
And fell upon a Blue-Tailed Sprite*
Pulling her shell
On the sands by his knee

She winked up and said
Fear not your wishes have been heard
Look to the east
By the tall tattooed tree*

So the sailor sat down
His eyes exploring every surf
Casting like nets
Through the waves in the sea

On a day that was clear
He saw an angel growing tall
Coming to find him
And set his soul free

Now today all his friends
Sit 'round and toast to Jack McKay
Lost in a storm
Off the Coast of Tripoli*

On the day of his birth
They raise a cup and dry their eyes
And bid him fair winds
Where ever he might be

*(Bond) an Indonesian port of call
* (Cat Napper Tree) a shady tree for cat napping
* (Blue-Tailed Sprite) a small blue snail that is common to the East Indies and makes its home in discarded shells

* (tattooed tree) a tree that has messages carved into it
*(Coast of Tripoli) the largest city of Libya, on a point of rocky land projecting into the Mediterranean Sea and forming a bay

A FIRST TIME MEETING

Your smile is captivating
When I look at you
It pleases my eyes

I listen to your voice
And even though we have never met
I have heard it many times
Somewhere, sometime not too long ago

I feel easy
Almost entranced
As my voice fails me

There is warmth
That surrounds you
And as the chilly of the evening comes near
I wonder if I might warm myself
In the fire of your glow

UNTIL ALL THE LEAVES FALL AGAIN

While my house slept silently
I stepped from the doorway
Into a cold October night
With the sweetening scent of autumn
And fresh fragrance of dying leaves
Dancing all about me

The wind guided me to that special place
A place where you and I always met
Only to find nothing
But a scattering of summer
Tossed haphazardly on the ground

I know that you have gone home
Back to the city lights and sounds of traffic
But next year
When we gather for summer
And the barn fires burn high
Touching the stars
I shall return here
To the sound of trees bursting with life
The stars falling into the morning
When the leaves of autumn come again

PATTY'S UNDERPANTS

Though she left
Hours ago
Just lying there
Over the bedroom chair
Hanging leisurely
As if to say
Good morning

MOVING MEDITATION

I watched for hours
As a piece of paper
Danced in the wind
Moving gently along the ground
Then suddenly
Tossed into the air
Before floating down
Again and again
Only to dance once more
Along the ground
With the wind

WALLS

You should have been an architect
Surrounding yourself with walls
So perfectly built
To withstand
All the love
I could possibly give you

A COLD NIGHT OF PERFECTION

That last night we spent together
I tried to tell you
With all the beautiful words I knew
How wonderful and perfect it was
Before saying
Goodbye

THE PERFECT WOMAN

She was everything
Any man could ever want
Young
Beautiful
Intelligent
Happy
Naked

FUNDAMENTALS OF A BUSTED RELATIONSHIP

She didn't call last night
… Perfect!

THE PERFECT DAY

Perfect!
She's no longer here
To tell me
What my problems are

WHAT TO DO WHEN IT RAINS

Cloudy day
I watched while the rain fell
Listening to the rhythm
Beating on my roof
In four-four time
… so I danced

LIKE HIM

His love for her was so deep
And so strong
That he would never allow her
To fall in love with a fool
Like him

WATCHING THE RIVER RUN

I keep watching the river run
Always twisting
Always turning
It's there I sit
Beneath your eyes
And mull over dreams of paradise
With you
Someplace where the sky is white and blue
Yet I'm thinking much too much
And I hate walking alone
It's not often that I ponder such
But when I wander
Thoughts come rushing in
Willy-nilly
I don't have a special place
Where all these thoughts begin
From the left
And from the right

Without warning
They attack me when I wake
Early in the morning
I wish I knew what I had done
So I'll sit here
With you standing there beside me
Beneath your eyes
Beneath the skies
Where clouds and birds and angels fly
And listen to the waters running free
As you watch me
Watching the river run

ACROSS AN EMPTY FIELD

She had a way of moving
Like a shadow against an open field
A way of floating over sharp words
And offhanded innuendos

Her smile always seemed to cover
A broad range of subjects
With a meaning that came across
As a wall of steel or gentle invitation

When she gave herself away
Even for a night, it was completely
And when she had gone
All that was left was a shadow
Moving across an empty field

WHEN SHE WAS GONE

I could hear her voice calling to me
From those dark secret places
Places I had been with her
A very long time ago

I could see her eyes looking at me
Whenever the wind blew lonely
Especially on the sleepless nights
When my dreams wandered away

Most of all
I could feel the way she loved me
Even when I was alone
And she was gone

THE CHILD WITHIN

Cold wind blew
Cold rain fell
While inside my country cottage
The furnace kicked in
And the warm air circulated around the room

This was supposed to be spring
But looking outside from my window
On a chilly and cloudy mid-April day
With a nor'easter bearing down on the Catskills
And the temperature barely above thirty-two
I knew that the real spring
Was still a long way off

Pulling up a chair by the window
With hot coffee and rising steam
I sat for most of the morning hours
Drawing pictures on my fogged window
Remembering times as a child
I would breathe onto the cold window panes
And do the same

In a way
It made me feel wonderful
Almost young again
With memories of winter

That came rushing back
Bringing a childish smile to an old man's face

THE TRUTH OF LIES

Here's the truth
I've told you lies
So you would love me more

But I don't like hiking
And I don't like dancing
Truth is I'm quite the bore

Still, I've learned to hike
And dance a bit
But if I had to do it again

I would take a new stance
To get into your pants
Find a way that is less of a strain

MORNING OF REFLECTED LIGHT

This was a morning of reflected light
Off the teacups
Dangling from the cupboard hooks
While down the hall
Several voices in conversation could be heard
Around an old breakfast table
In a country kitchen

This was a morning of reflected light
That returned youthful memories
From when as a child
The smell of coffee and hot buttered toast
Seemed to permeate the air
Smells
That have since thinned through the years
Along with voices in the old tongues

This was a morning of reflected light
That played off the old read books
That lined the shelves
That covered the walls
That were no longer read

This was a morning of reflected light
That danced on five dusty guitars
And off the hands of an old musician
Who enjoyed the music
That was no longer played

This was a morning of reflected light
And for all its sadness
The memories it allowed
Made it a most wonderful morning

GOD CAN TELL

She had lost mountains and rivers
On rainy paths through sunny fields
Golden chains and lover's kisses
Hidden secrets unrevealed

Lost in years of sun-drenched grasses
Watching buildings rise and fall
Recollections of her childhood
Places lost she couldn't recall

She mislaid her youthful fervor
And that smile I knew so well
A fighter once, now an observer
Caught between heaven and hell

Now she stands like those before her
Some who've risen, some who fell
She has questions needing answers
That only God can tell

THE OBITUARY OF JOHN PAGE

Beloved by his town
He had suddenly passed on
The obituary read he was gone

His family decided a theater in town
Would be used since the man was renown

So they rented the theater
And placed him for view
Come pay your respects to John Page

The newspaper said
That for only one night
His body will appear "live" on stage

NOTHING LEFT TO SEE

Everything he knew was gone
Except what were his memories
The future and the dawn had merged
And passed away to history
He came to realize that fate
Had given him no guarantee
No foes to best or place to rest
No strength to fight or flee
So if you think you might have seen
Someone that looked a bit like me
With unsung deeds
Wish him Godspeed
For now there's nothing left to see

DAYS OF YOUTH AND FISH

Fishing was a joy
A way to let time float by
Every weekend with his St. Croix in hand
He would take a leisurely walk to the lake
And as he did for over fifty years
Fly fish

It was always the act
Not the catch
That was his way of letting the world
Fade magically away

Still… these last several years
The lake had been quiet and still
And try as he did
All the fish seemed to be… gone

There were times as a boy
When bite by bite
The crowded lake, filled with fish
Would grab the hook
Until forced to stop by the weight of the load
He would lie on the cool green grass
And enjoy the summer sun

But those were the days of youth and fish
When the earth was still warmed by the sun
We've taken so much and given back less
Those days are long since gone

DREAMS OF MARY ANNE

I stand before my open door
And watch a wicked northeast wind

My eyes can tell it's loud as hell
But I can't hear a God damned thing

There are some benefits to age
My hearing has in years grown dim

The storm may pound and thunder sound
But I'm going back to bed again
So as I watch the pounding rain
And wonder when this storm began

My thoughts disperse as I immerse
Into my dreams of Mary Anne

BRIGHT EYES

I don't remember what she wore
Or even said when we first met
What I remember were her eyes
So deep and blue and calling

I'm not the kind that lightly feels
Emotions that I've laid to rest
Still what I felt can't be denied
She had me lost within bright eyes

DREAMS OF THE IMMIGRANT

With dreams, plans and skills
With hammers and drills
They all came from far distant shores

In stories they told
There were streets made of gold
In a country with wide opened doors

If they worked hard and learned
With the wages they earned
Opportunity was always there

And within this small place
That they came to embrace
Some of them became millionaires

To their daughters and sons
They chose not to share
The language from where they had come

They chose not to hint
That they were immigrants
So their children weren't called foreign scum

So two generations on
For what their parents have done
They were welcome to these open shores

But their legacies were gone
It was not learned or passed on
With traditions they were taught to ignore

IT'S A MIRACLE

A single snowflake
Falling
Falling
Falling
Falling on the tongue of a small child
Playing outside
In winter

It's a miracle

HOBO'S STORY

Dark streets lost past rain-drenched houses
Shadows looking for a home
I've been here in a thousand places
Nameless faces so well-known
Somewhere there are lovers kissing
Down these dark filled alleyways
I can hear their whispers carry
Through this fog-filled blackened maze
Sleeping forms just inches from me
In warm blankets filled with news
Yesterdays abandoned stories
Fending off the cold with booze
Time to choose a spot to rest in
Just a place to lay my head
At least until a new day's dawning
Wakes me from my pauper's bed

THE SCENT OF WINTER

I could smell the sunlight
Fragrantly falling
Like a morning perfume
Over winter's skin
Sinking into the pores of the earth
As it sped along its way

I watched as the trees
Lifted their noses into the air
And waved their arms about
Endlessly trying to reach the sky
As if to say
Good morning

LOOKING FOR SOMEONE LIKE ME

My back's filled with pain
And keeps telling my brain
That walking these days ain't much fun
My dentures are loose
Cause I've lost every tooth
And the food that I eat I just gum
My hands look quite old
That happens I'm told
When we get very far up in years
There are parts that still grow
I am sure that you know
By the size of my very large ears
Now sleeping is a chore
And I do tend to snore
But that all comes along with my age
My memory's quite thin
And my hearing is dim
I can barely eke out minimum wage
So if you're like me
And would like company
You can give me a call on the phone
In the white pages you'll find
Under old and benign
Folks like me in the old soldiers' home

MORNING OF ONE

It was a lazy morning
A morning of slow stretches
And leisurely yawns
A morning of slow motion
And coffee that took forever
To pour into a bottomless cup

It was a lazy morning
A morning when the sun
Took most of the day
Just to get high into the heavens
And the birds hung in the air
Like balloons in a windless sky

It was a most lazy morning
Feeling you wake beside me
And our bodies entwine
For what seemed like
Days upon days upon days

As together
In an everlasting moment
Of an everlasting lazy morning
We were one

MERRY CHRISTMAS

Good morning she said
As she walked through the door
Greeted by two purring cats

Good morning they said
In courteous reply
May we please take your coat and your hat

So she sat on the sofa
Near a book of the sea
While the cats sat beside her and offered Brandy

Which she gladly accepted
And put in her cup
With three lumps of sugar and a bright buttercup

That she mixed altogether
And drank straight away
While the ships in the harbor pulled into the bay

She opened the windows
To smell the salt sea
Then she sat as her cats hopped upon both her knees

And they purred out this song
As they watched her get tight
Merry Christmas to all and to all a good night

THERE'S CHRISTMAS IN YOUR EYES

I can see Christmas in your eyes
And jingle bells dropping from the trees
So loud
I cannot shout above them

If you cannot hear me
What does it matter if I say
I love you
My words are lost
In the ringing

In the sound
Of Christmas
In the sound of jingle bells
In the sound of quiet trees
Lost in the forest

IN THE MIND OF THE BEHOLDER

He kept getting the order wrong
As I turned to my date and said
What a dumb waiter!

That's not a dumb waiter she replied
I have a dumb waiter in my house
And it doesn't look anything like him!

It was at this point
When I began to think
What a dumb date!

ALONE IN THE DARK

I almost went to sleep
Without remembering you

And just for that moment
I was at peace
With the night

SHE KNEW, SHE KNEW, SHE KNEW

She was waiting for him
Long before she knew
She was waiting for him

She was in love with him
Long before she knew
She was in love with him

She knew his touch
Long before
She knew his touch

She knew
Long before
She knew
She knew

TO SHARE IT ALL WITH YOU

I love to dance
To lost music
And rummage
Through the rooms
Of old houses
That have long since
Been torn down

Out
In wildflower fields
Hand in hand
I watched
As our breath
Stolen by laughter
Filled the dreams we had
Of places we wished to be

While I watched her belly dance
To the beat of wild drums
I wondered
If maybe someday
She might dance with me
To the sound
Of lost music
That echoed through the rooms
Of old houses
That were torn down
Long, long ago

ALONE IN THE DARK

I almost went to sleep
Without remembering you

And just for that moment
I was at peace
With the night

THE COLOR OF PICASSO

The wind blows
Like a paint brush
And though
I would like to tell you
How much I love you
I'm too stoned
And anything I say
Would probably sound
Like a Picasso painting
On acid

ALMOST A VERY GOOD YEAR

It was the year of the dark yellow moon
When the cold winds came
And the oceans turned green
Before running out from shore

It was the dawdling year
A year sadness fell from our eyes
Like an eruption of hammering storms
The type we kept in the gardens
Just around the block
By the Stop and Shop

It was the year the dog died
The year we placed him on a board
And all the children wore black
Carrying him home
Like a soldier returning from war

It was the year you packed my lunch
Sending me off to work
Wearing your "I've got a secret" smile
In that new dress you bought on Monday
That flowed about you like a cloud

It was the year I came home
Only to find you had gone
Leaving nothing but the rains
And a note that said
It was almost a very good year

CAMEL CIGARETTES

It was determined
That his lung cancer
Came from the finest blend
Of Turkish & domestic tobaccos
That did not allow for
Premiums or coupons
As the cost of the tobaccos
Blended in Camel cigarettes
Prohibits the use of them

WHEN THE LEAVES FALL

While my house slept silently
I stepped from the doorway
Into a cold October night
With the sweetening scent of autumn
And fresh fragrance of dying leaves
Dancing all about me

The wind guided me to that special place
A place where you and I always met
Only to find nothing
But a scattering of summer
Tossed haphazardly on the ground

I know that you have gone home
Back to the city lights and sounds of traffic
But next year
When we gather for summer
And the barn fires burn high
Touching the stars
I shall return here
To the sound of trees bursting with life
The stars falling into the morning
When the leaves of autumn come again

A NAKED HOUSE

In a naked house
Echoing with the sound
Of a ticking clock
Traffic
From an open window
And the hum
Of an old refrigerator

In a naked house
Silence resonates
Off empty walls
Following her
From room to room
With the click
Of wooden heels

In a naked house
She walks about
Listening for a voice
That no longer speaks
The words of love
She longs to hear

In a naked house
She walks
Day and night
Searching for a memory
She will never find

PASSING INTO SPRING

Like a caterpillar changing into a butterfly
I saw the final weeks of winter
Shed its cocoon

In undulating movements
Winters shell slowly and almost invisibly
Fell away into a metamorphosis of beauty

I watched as spring tested its wings
Emerging and spreading
Into greens, blues, yellows and reds

While inside the little town of Woodstock
People began to appear with smiling eyes
Sniffing at the cool clean air

And the once smoky chimneys
That fought so bravely against winter's cold
One by one… fell fast asleep

THE TRUTH HAS NOT SET ME FREE

So very slowly
Over days, months and years
I have wanted someone to come into my life
But at the end of each day
Tired
Achy
Hungry
I come home only to eat and rest and sleep
I have come home alone

Whenever the chance appears
And I come across someone
Who may be that someone I am looking for
And I share with them my feelings
They listen
They smile
And then they run… saying
You're coming on way too fast!

But at age 61
I can't play the waiting game anymore
Because tomorrow may never come
And all that I have to offer
Are my todays

SHE DREAMS OF DAYS TO COME

The sweet smell of spring
Danced on the autumn winds
Under the eaves of the wooden cottage
Past the old rusted screens
Filling the room with fragrance
From the flowers that hid from view

Out past the garden
And far beyond
Into the dense green forest
That guarded the old house
From the music of fierce songbirds
That sang in the morning sun
She dreams of days to come

Though he cannot see her
Or hear the laughter
That comes when she thinks of him
Nor does he know that today
She wears her summer blue dress
Because he loved the way it fell
Across the curves of her body

Today the day will be brighter
The sky will be bluer
And the earth will turn more gently
Because she knows he thinks of her
Thinking of him
And like her he dreams
Of days to come

CONSTANTINOPLE

Constantinople haunts my nights
In dreams both sad and stirring
Of wooden ships
Under star-filled skies
Searching for fortunes
Hidden by those long gone

As we sail away
Down the dark Euphrates
Shadowy eyes
Filled with lost dreams
Can be seen in the sadness
Of the forgotten
Waiting on the shrouded banks
Forever

Looking back
Toward the city lights
Reaching up
To the night sky
Constantinople waits
And waits
And waits
For me
And for you
To come

NEVER TO BE HEARD FROM AGAIN

Last night
As I watched the moonlight
Dance over the woodland fields
Casting soft-lit shadows
As it carelessly fell
Through the forest trees
I remembered other nights

Nights
When the two of us
Would sit
On the front porch
Looking at the starlit skies
In the warmth of summer

I could still hear
Your sweet soft voice
Filled with declarations of love
And beautiful words
Unraveling like a child's ribbon
That had be thrown
Haphazardly on the ground

Your words
That I now see
Were only meant to please me
For a night
Running from you
Like a soft warm river

Your words
That I watched falling
Like honey
Down the gentle curves
Of your body
Before disappearing into the wind
And just like you
At the rising of the new day
Never to be heard from again

FIREFLIES

When I was a young boy
I would sit on my front porch
In the summer nights
And watch the fireflies
Dance their dance around the trees
To a young boy In New York City
It was magical
Seventy years later
I wait for them to return
But it's been a long, long time
Since I have seen a firefly
In New York City

1:43 IN THE MORNING

At 1:43 in the morning
I sit here thinking of you
And wonder
Are you still beautiful

Are you sleeping
Or with somebody else
Do you ever think of me
The way I think of you

At 1: 43 in the morning
Does your life have any meaning
Is there someone to catch you
If you stumble or fall

I don't love you any less
Just because you've gone
But it's 1: 43 in the morning
And I can't sleep

So I lie here
In the quiet of the night
With the rain that seems to forever fall
And I wonder… yes, I wonder
If you're still beautiful

HE STILL WHISPERS

There are signs
Which tell me that you've been here
Uncontrollable signs
Like my repeating your name out loud
Over and over
Or the carefully folded corner
Of a book that you left
Unfinished
Some of these I can remove
While others that remain
Like my heart
You have taken far away
And though I have promised
To never speak your name again
Occasionally
When no one can hear
I still whisper

TOMORROWS

She was Breathtaking
With an ass that you could see the future in
And me
Always wanting to know the future

LIKE A WHISPER IN THE WIND

Today the leaves fell
While the rain tumbled down
Uncaring, indiscriminately on all below

As the earth turned so did the weather

I watched from my window
As summer leisurely fled south
Down the old roads
Roads that it had so often traveled
And knew so well

Off to the north
A wind with the chill of winter
Told stories of the coming cold

And my window
Which always opened to the warmth of the sun
Remained closed giving me shelter

I remember
When I was much younger
That years lasted forever
And seasons fought the onslaught of change

These days
The years fly like an eagle
And are gone like a whisper in the wind

FALLEN DREAMS

There are no more summers
Or winters, or springs
I have fallen into autumn
And as I look at my outstretched arms
I can see that my leaves are quickly falling

All about me the world sleeps
In preparation of rebirth
Flowers, cars and trees
Hide beneath a blanket
Of pure white newly fallen snow

As my house sits quietly
Lying in the shadow of the night
My cats circle round and round
Finally falling into themselves
As their tiny bodies jiggle and jerk
In a land of feline dreams
While the only dreams left to me
Are those that cannot see beyond autumn

ARCTIC DREAMS

Cold winter wind
Ice-covered leaves
Crackling loudly underfoot
While the still, still forest
Sways silently
With the songs
Of frozen birds

In the solitude
Of the Catskills
Our voices
Evaporate
Like a mountain fog
Pushed by the breath
Of winter's holy wind

I will wait
If I know you will come
Between the ice frozen flowers
And arctic dreams
Resting in fields
Of gentle memories
Waiting to bloom
In spring

EVERYONE GOES AWAY

There comes a time
(When that is I can't say)
When everyone, everywhere goes away
I often wonder why they can't stay
But I guess that's the way that it's been
Life's like the seasons
They come and they go
No, I don't mean the seasons
I mean those we know
Regardless of feelings
It's on with the show
While we hope that tomorrow will bring
A day to remember or new song to sing
Maybe a love that reminds us of spring
But what comes tomorrow
(I really can't say)
Will linger awhile it won't last a day
Like Macbeth or Hamlet
We have parts we must play
But all of us everywhere
Sooner or later
No matter how hard we might pray
Eventually, ultimately, in the finale
Everyone goes away

WHAT SHE WAS LIKE

She was like a shadow
That passes over a field of flowers
And just for that moment
Gives them reprieve from the sun
Or like a dream
That is so beautiful
That you want it to come
Again and again
And though it never returns
It will be a dream
That you will never forget
A dream
That you tell others about
Not that you want to share it
But in the telling
It helps you remember it
Forever

THE SHADOWS OF TINKER STREET

I watched
As the long winter shadows
Grew past the travelers on the green
Touching the tinker street stores

Like an actor in a play
The evening light dimmed
While the early night lights appeared
One by one by one
Lighting up
All the stores on Tinker Street

As I listened
To the sound of music and drums
Filter past the growing crowd
The local Tinker Street musicians
Gathered once again
For another evening's performance

All these things painted a picture
As I watched a mystical vision
Of shadows and visitors and musicians
And of course the townsfolk
Swirl and mix into the Woodstock night

It was flawless
The perfect country street
Magically remembering its roots
And passing them on
During a dreamy cool wintry night
All to the delight
Of Tinker Street

A GIFT OF CIRCLES

Her smell lingers
And her voice echoes
Down the empty hallways

Try as I might
She has left behind
Shadows
Shadows that speak to me
And move in the visions
Of everything about

As I watch these specters
Roam freely about the house
All with the same face
Filled with joy and laughter
I wonder where she has gone
And why she had gone

I am left
With only a voice
On a phone machine
Saying her farewells
With tears that drip soundlessly
On the dry, dry ground

Tears that in spring
Have brought forth
Flowers
Tears that in spring
Have restored my faith
In the circle of love

WHAT COFFEE CAN NEVER REPLACE

It finally came
The last grass manicure of the season
As the tall jagged leaves
That once dotted the landscape
Now lay flat
Browning in the cool warm sun

Once again
Autumn had crept upon me
With the smell of colors in the air
And the taste of hot coffee
To chase the cold mornings away

Although
Not long ago
It was you
Who was my morning cup
It was you
Who chased away the cold night air
And it was you
Whose taste warmed me and filled me
With a love
That I fear
Morning coffee can never replace

IS THERE A SOUL?

Is there a soul that cannot fly
Who's never seen a star-filled sky
Or felt the joys of falling rain
Or known true love they couldn't attain

A soul that's never seen the light
Or shared love's warmth on cold dark nights
A soul that's never seen the sun
Or joined their heart with anyone

A soul whose spirit cannot soar
Or didn't know what a kiss was for
A soul whose heart cannot forgive
Somewhere within this world we live

I pray that they can shed their pain
That they might hopefully attain
Whatever they have never known
And know that they are not alone

WITHOUT REGRETS

The winter winds blowing through the chimes
Sounded like a Sunday morning at the Vatican
All about the house
The ringing continued throughout the night

All this
As the air, so very cold
And the heater working nonstop
Barely kept the warmth from fading

Sitting at the computer
I passed the sleepless hours
Going back through some old pictures
And came upon some photos you and me

I have seen the changes over the years
Yes, you are as beautiful as ever
But in these pictures was a smile
A smile that I haven't seen for a long time
A smile that somewhere between then and now
You have placed safely out of view

I know
That I will never be the one
To make you smile that way again
But I can see your hand upon the key
That will open the lock to your heart
Dear one (as you often say) I rejoice with you
He has a sweet kindness about him
And I am happy for those feelings he awoke in you

I can see from the way he looks at you
And you at him
That there is something special between you
Please don't let that fly away
Abandon yourselves for a night
And share each other's love
The only regrets you will have is if you don't
And a life without regrets
Is a life… not worth living

FALLEN DREAMS

There are no more summers
Or winters, or springs
I have fallen into autumn
And as I look at my outstretched arms
I can see that my leaves are quickly falling

All about me the world sleeps
In preparation of rebirth
Flowers, cars and trees
Hide beneath a blanket
Of pure white newly fallen snow

As my house sits quietly
Lying in the shadow of the night
My cats circle round and round
Finally falling into themselves
As their tiny bodies jiggle and jerk
In a land of feline dreams
While the only dreams left to me
Are those that cannot see beyond autumn

WHERE DREAMS AND RIVERS FLOW

There is a land that waits for me
Between the forest and the sea
Where mountains reign and never fall
And eagles answer to the call
Where trees grow taller than the sun
And all the sadness is undone
So come by me as I must go
To where my dreams like rivers flow

TOMORROW TODAY

I have lost too many today's
And cannot get back to the place
From where I had started
Or to the place where I should be

No matter how many days I stay awake
There is no way to catch up
Or replace all that is missing
Or lost

So today
I shall leave all that I have lost
Behind

Today is the beginning
And I will believe that tomorrow
Is no different
Than today… if it comes

EVEN EAGLES FALL

Like an eagle on broken wings
She flies through the day
On shattered dreams

Through once clear crystal eyes
The world ebbs and fades into view

The sky
Once filled with eagle calls
Now quiet remembrances
Of long-gone times

While heavens splendor
Filled with billowed clouds
Does not reply as she sings

Only the earth
Waits to embrace
Each flight and day that passes
As the sky falls away
And the earth draws near
'Til embraced by the soft green grasses

WHEN ALL MY WORDS HAVE RUN AWAY

Sometimes it's like trying to write
With a pencil made of glass
Nothing comes
And I think
There are no more poems left
Inside of me
Even though I try
The words I chose
Run like water off of the paper
And I wonder
What shall I do
When all my poems are gone
And all my words have run away

HEAVEN'S GATE

Death and darkness heed me not
I will not wait for you to call
Come if you will before daylight
And give me dignity to fall

I am no longer young with smiles
I cannot change what's gone before
Nor can I fill the darkened night
Or open closed past sealed doors
So here I sit with wonderment
Is there still time for me to change?
And find a place in heaven's gate
Where I might enter once again

IT'S TRUE

I have some secrets
Dark and deep
Where light can't go
And hearts can't sleep

A place where dreams
Cannot reside
And darkness has
No place to hide

I'd thought I learned
To see the light
And cast out fears
That filled my night

I'd thought I learned
To hide my fears
And took the time
To shed my tears

But somewhere deep
Within these eyes
Are tears unshed
I need to cry

When worries past
Are put aside
And tears for past mistakes
Are cried… it's true
When all's been said and done and tried
No matter what I'd done or did or do
In the end I'm still in love with you

MY LOVE

If my love were a bird
It could never fly
Or a song
That no one could sing
If my love were tears
They would hide in my eyes
Or a beautiful bell
That couldn't ring

If my love was a story
It could never be told
For no voice
Could hold that much pain
And if my love
Was the sun above
It would fall from the sky
Like the rain

THINGS CHANGE

I watched from my window
As the winds blew back
To a time when I was still free

I could see myself playing
As a child in a world
That was boundless with places to see

Now as an old man
My hopes and ambitions
Linger behind lock and key

What visions remain
Are nowhere the same
As the dreams in my youth used to be

I CAN NO LONGER UNDERSTAND

I stood under the freezing sun
And watched the frozen rivers run
Through sharpened rocks past shivering deer
Whose eyes shed ice-cold winter tears
And wondered why spring didn't arrive
To help the trees and plants revive
I'd hoped to leave my children more
Than darkened times and frightening wars
I can no longer understand
What's happened to our glorious land

IT'S RAINING DREAMS

I looked outside my window
As a torrent of dreams fell
All about the land
From a dark clouded sky

I recognized some of them
Suddenly realizing
That others like me
Had the same dreams

For quite some time
I watched
As they landed all about me
Unfolding one by one

Until I came to realize
That dreams must be nurtured
And tended to
Like a seed in fertile earth

But when it came
To tending my dreams
I was not the right farmer
To help them grow

GABBY

Through a looking glass
With a quizzing gaze
She stares at me
Her camera eyes
And enchanting smile
Behind the reflection
Of a restaurant window
On a Woodstock road
To bacon and eggs

BLACKOUT

It was a typical Woodstock blackout
All homes east
Appeared like an ebony backdrop
Against a plutonian sky
The once familiar door of my home
Dissolved into a mysterious portal
I continually found myself
Exclaiming profanities
While my nose found walls
I'd previously ignored
My cats lovingly came
To assist me tripping several times
As my nose and rug collaborated
Meanwhile my dog didn't bark

ANGELS FLY WITH DRAGONS WINGS

I found a place where raindrops sing
And angels fly with Dragons' wings
Where rings of fire can be heard
And sadness is an unknown word
Within a sea of boundless tales
I found a ship with weathered sails
Where morals never interfere
With thoughts of love both far and near
I still can hear the voices call
Of those whose bodies I've seen fall
Whose names I often call to mind
Of better times I'd left behind
There was a time when I was king
And angels flew with Dragons' wings
There was a time when friends replied
Whose voices I still keep inside

FACES

The drenching rains came
And the once soft brook
Now a mighty torrent
Sought an easy path
Through the undergrowth
Bouncing past cast-iron trees
That refused to concede
While I sat in my home
By the safety of the fire
Remembering stories
Of similar days
And faces long gone
In the folds
Of time and rain

FINGERED WINGS

There was a boy with fingered wings
Whose hands could see the strangest things
On seamless foaming frothing tides
In narrow corridors that hide
The secrets of the fears that bind
Or truth so bright that it could blind
Where only touch may understand
A minor mystery so grand
About a broken fingered wing
That try and fail, couldn't see a thing

GROUPS MINUS ONE

(From a dictionary of animal groups)

A tribe of goats
A sleuth of bears
A rag of colts
A down of hares

A brace of ducks
A cloud of gnats
A clash of bucks
A clutter of cats

A shiver of sharks
A swarm of flies
An ascension of larks
A tiding of magpies

A drift of hogs
A gaggle of geese
A colony of frogs
A mess of meese

SNOW DROPS

Snowflakes gathered haphazardly on the window sill
As a child's eyes studied the mounting shapes
He loved to watch the snow fall, it was a reprieve
From having to go outside in the cold
Some days he wished it would snow forever
But even as happiness filled him
The weather turned and the flurry quietly stopped
He hated the heavy coat cussing softly as it went on
Hat, coat and rubber boots the gear of a snow shoveler
He was a boy out to do battle with winter
Worse now the sun made a spotted appearance
Causing the snow to slowly melt
Watching the drops of water along the roof's edge
Unhurriedly gathering and growing about to fall
He stood transfixed while watching snowdrops

SHE'S GONE

On the Woodstock green sitting on a bench
She doesn't see me watching
Traffic on Tinker Street
Hides me from her view
She skips about in a world of her own
Unaware of me across the street
Watching her laugh at the store windows
And smiling at everyone passing by
My eyes seem transfixed by her form
As she grows smaller in the distance
A noise from deep within my soul
Makes a cheerless silence of sound
Reviving memories too sharp to hold
And much too distant to touch.

MEN DON'T CRY

It's like rain when I remember you
The sun could be shining brightly
Yet moisture seems to fall
And I don't know why
I am sure that no one sees me
I have places that I hide
I was told as a child that men don't cry
I try not to bother others
It would be a sign of weakness
Never say, suggest or otherwise imply
That my feelings overwhelm me
In the night when I sit lonely
You see, as a child I was told that men don't cry
Since I left you I have been drifting
Now it seems there's no salvation
I can't return or make these tears run dry
And the lessons of my childhood
Have lost their secret meaning
I don't understand the reason men don't cry

THE TOUCH OF LOVE

No matter where I am
Or where I go
You are always there
I can feel you touch me
As close as the air
In every breath that I take

Time has taken my youth
And in its place
Has given me memories
Filled with melancholy
Of your love and beauty

Little by little
I have felt my strength and life
Ebb from my body
But not my memories
They have only grown stronger
Along with my love
For you

RICHARD BRAUTIGAN

I find myself
Reading a dead man's poems
And wondering
If he'll have time
To talk with me

THE WORLD'S FASTEST CAT

Driving to work
Through a busy town
Skit-scat a cat came running
Across the road
His quickness was undeniable
Like lightning through a wire
Past speeding cars
And racing trucks
With my own eyes I saw
The world's fastest flat cat

BUDDHA BASED SOUP

A touch of faith
A pinch of hope
Add compassion
Hold the pope
It may seem odd
Or even strange
Mix what you want
Then wait for change

LAMPLIGHT STORM

In a pitch-black world at midnight
From my bedroom window
A snowstorm leaps and dances
Under a streetlamp's glow
As the world fades away
From the borders of light
I watch a miracle of nature
Cascading onto the pavement
A blizzard of falling snow
Dropping softly
In a streetlight world

ORIGAMI

She would fold, refold then fold again
And from the paper arose a swan
I was always amazed at what she did
A creation of beauty from paper
She would fold, refold then fold again
And from her heart arose a song
A creation of beauty from hope and faith
And like the swan she helped me fly

SHE WAITS FOR SPRING

On a snow-covered mound
Near a gray frozen river
At a table where there should be none
Winter's jacket is wrapped
About her frail figure
Measuring deeds she had done
Not feeling the cold or the sun
And waits for the river to run

SUDDENLY BEAUTIFUL

Her head bowed and eyes down
In a dress so plain it fell into the wall
A woman of unapparent features sat
While all about her others were dancing
Still… nobody seemed to look her way
Halfway through the night with many gone
The music whispered two words to her
Come dance
The notes begging over and over
To leave her space of isolation
A calling that slowly became a feeling
That unexpectedly made her rise
With exquisite movements
Her body found itself in delicacy
Stopping all about her
Each eye hoping that someday
They might be as wonderful
And as she danced
She found herself
Suddenly beautiful

THOSE MAGIC TIMES

The memories of my life
Are not real
They are filled with beauty
And melting colors
Of how I choose
To recall the times
That have been swallowed
By the days of my youth

Those wonderful times
Once forgotten empty spaces
My mind has filled
With new stories
Of how I prefer
To remember life

As I look back
Over my life of stories
I have some wondrous tales
That I have told for so long
That even I
Now believe
They are true

A TESTAMENT OF HOPE

Twisted and bent
My tired hands
With crooked fingers
Painfully write beautiful poems

My words have found a home
Here
On this paper you are holding
They have found a place to rest

Lately
My voice
No longer carries my words
Nor can it convey the passion
I had once felt
When I had written them

It's as though
They were placed here
Waiting for you
To raise them from the dead
And bring them back to life

These days
I have chosen my final road
With care
And though my end draws near
I see many blank papers
Waiting alongside the road
To record my journey

There will be no sorrow here
No tales of woe
Or love's lost stories

There will be no pity me's
Or hate to find along the way
Or even sadness
For deeds past done

Instead
I shall tell you of my dreams
Which until the final step
I still hope to fill
And of my love
That until the very end
I still hope to find

BEDROOM WINTER

There is winter in the room
As frozen shadows fall
Across an empty bed

Words lie about
Still and silent

Words
That can never
Be taken back

No matter
How many blankets
She covers herself in

There will never be enough
To warm
An empty heart

AMALGAMATE

I was blinded
By the shadows
And deafened
By the silence
That surrounded us

While the years
That have quietly passed
Thundering
Tear at my heart
When I realized
That you had gone

It was only a night
That we shared
So fleeting
And yet this night remained
A single night
That continues
To go on and on and on

You have taken with you
A part of me
A part
I do not want you to return
But I too
Have taken and kept
A part of you

WHAT THE SEA HAS TAKEN

Sometimes
When the northern winds
Blow cold and still
And St. Elmo's fire
Blazes in the night sky

Sometimes
When flying fish
Scurry about the darkness
Over the cold North Sea
Casting dolphin shadows
On the icy waters

I think of you
Thinking of me
And wonder
Why the sea
Has taken you
Away

IN LIEU OF PASSION

It was a dry winter
And as the months passed
Without rain or snow
I watched the cold rivers descend
And small springs disappear

The waters
Once quick and sparkling
Now ran listlessly
Down and through the old mountains
And across the parched brown fields

Still
The people came
To feel the wind
As they ran and danced
On the dry mounds
Of crumbling leaves

And although the earth
Appeared old and dry
We knew
In the dark of night
Just like us, when we awake
She would soon explode
With the beauty of spring

I have longed for your shining eyes
To guide me through my confrontations
And the sound of your voice
In the dark, dark nights
That could quiet my rising temptations

I once found peace
With the work of my hands
And relief
In the comfort of slumber

But those days have passed
And all that remains
Are the visions of your sleeping form
In the quiet of my bedroom

IN THE QUIET OF WINTER'S SILENCE

Night inched its way
Up the north-east side
Of my house
Much in the way
A little child
Would climb over a fence
One small hand at a time

And as night's shadow
Reached the very top
It stopped for a moment
Before tumbling over
And falling down
The south-west wall
Plunging the house into darkness

It was a familiar winter night
But what I remember most
Was how much colder it seemed
Then other winters before
Nonetheless
Warm or cold
It was winter
Complete in every way
With winds like icy fingers
And falling snow
That seemed to go on and on
Forever

It was on a night like this
That I thought of you
A night
When I was overwhelmed
By everything that winter was
Compounded by a darker darkness
Than any nights I could remember
That had come before

And try as I might
I could not summon the sun
Or make it rise more swiftly
To free my mind
From unwanted thoughts
Nor could I find any solace
In the quiet, quiet
Of winter's silence

A PAPER CALLS

Here
Upon this blank paper
My words have found a home
A place to rest and say hello
To you

It's almost as if
The words were placed here
Waiting for your eyes
To find them
And give them life

I have thought about this
Maybe it's a magic paper
That was left behind
By some old
And ancient sorcerer

Who cast a powerful spell
Giving whatever poet
Who found it
The power to make
Their words come alive

Or maybe it was just
A plain old piece of paper
Whose emptiness inspired me
To take pen in hand
And write a poem for you

I have thought about this
For quite some time
After all
What true poet could let
Such an invitation pass by

In the end
I have come to realize
That every blank paper
Is just a poem
Whose words have not yet come

CONFLICTED!

She would parade about the house
With a grin
That went from ear to ear
Flaunting herself
Without so much as
A stitch of clothes on
From the waist down
Taking poses
That would make Penthouse Magazine
Burst into flame
Forcing me
Let me repeat that…
"FORCING ME" to watch
And God knows
How difficult and terrible it was
For me to be put
In such a challenging situation
I hated every single minute
That I didn't have enough time
To look

A Poem Of Frozen Birds

It was an unexpected chill
As the icy north wind
Pierced like a shooting needle
Through the morning sun
So cold
That you could almost see it
Tumble down the mountainside

It was a morning of frozen birds
Falling like rain from the sky
Off the boughs of trees
Dripping down
And splashing like colored drops
On the rock-hard ground

As I walked the wintry woods
I pictured the ice-cold wind as a brush
Painting the woods with drops of color
Bird colors of blues, greens and reds
That seemed to come alive
And sing

An Agreement of Love

An act of kindness unperceived
Love freely offered not received
A thoughtful deed to offer ease
Pain of words from those who tease
A kindly gesture from a friend
Advice and help from those who'll lend
A means and chance to help me mend
And lift me up lest I descend
When all was said I'd hoped you'd sway
And not dismiss these words away
At last we see and do agree
That I love you
And you don't love me

When It All Comes Together

To look at him
You would never know
It was the fragments of his life
That made him whole

Deer Prints In The Snow

No one else would notice
The little things he saw
An old letter
Or the romance books
He refused to throw away
It was these things
Kept as reminders
To an old heart
From a young time
Sort of like waking up
On a frosty
Snow-filled morning
You don't have to see them
To know they were here
Just look on the ground
And see the deer prints
In the snow

Paying Attention

The softer she spoke
The more he listened

It finally reached a point
Where she said nothing at all

And he totally understood
Everything

Beneath Streetlights

The one-eyed streetlight
Took dictation
To the hustle and bustle
Of the home below
Looking at
The moonlit trees
Watching people
Move to and fro
In a world
Where nothing's noticed
In a home
Where lamps still shine
The figures of
A loving couple
Go unobserved
Beneath the sky
With the exception of
A one-eyed streetlamp
Who watches over
Homes of light
Sharing itself
With unknown strangers
Chasing shadows
Into the night

Pieces Of Themselves

So small
With sleepy eyes
That kept puckering
Over and over

So perfect
Tiny fingers
That could barely
Hold a thumb

So happy
The two parents
Looking down
On the pieces of themselves

I Saw The Night Mysterious

Once when young
I saw the night mysterious
With moon and stars and lights in flight
It made me very curious
I thought the moon
So all alone
Amidst the stars that brightly shone
Reflected light that made me feel
Delirious
Until I realized
The feeling wasn't serious
But as I sit
I must admit
What lies ahead I can't predict
When daylight fades
And dark shades fall on us
I still can see the night mysterious

Faucet Eyes

Your eyes are dripping
Like a broken faucet
And I can't find
The right wrench
To fix
Your faucet eyes

One Of The Best

With a slight hobble
And a light in his eyes
That seemed to capture
The whole universe
In a single glance

Totally unnoticed
The old man watched
As on the grass
Young men practiced
The age-old arts

Smiling to himself
Content in knowing
There was a time
When he was one
Of the very best

Tears

For weeks she thought
After they split up
That she had left
Several things behind

He found them
On the very first day
In the corners
Of his eyes

Pieces Of November

It was the month from hell
Where everything fell apart
The one she loved had left
Her birthday went unnoticed
As little by little
All her hopes and dreams
Slowly began to fade away
The tears she shed so often
Could no longer be found
And the house she lived in
For so many years
No longer felt like a home
Gradually as the days past
A realization took hold
And an understanding
That all things bad
Must eventually pass
Placing a smile upon her face
Much in the way
A knight would don armor
She raised herself from sorrow
And slowly began to pick up
The pieces of November

Almost Good News

They thought he had
A rare disease
But the good news was
The autopsy came back
Negative

The Thievery Of Clouds

Can you see the moon dancing
In a night filled sky
With animal stars

While peacock meadows
Of blue and green
Call our names aloud

Perplexing how she smiles
As moonbeams of light
Roll over her

Be careful where you walk
You know how clouds
Can steal the view

Two Quarts Down

Like small animals
Scurrying about well-worn paths
Down empty highways
Rushing through flashing lights
Of reds, yellows and greens
Seeking familiar spaces
In places only known to them
They exchange winks
In lights of highs and lows
Hurrying to work or rest
And in these early times
Before the engine roared to life
He noticed that his car
Was bleeding

Sometimes You Have To Sing

He was dreaming and in his dream he saw
His very life rocked to its foundation
Looking up he noticed the roof of his home
Was badly leaking
Surely, this was an image
That needed no interpretation
There were those about him
But not the ones he loved
Telling him all their problems
Yet through all of this
He could hear a distant music
And the voice of a stranger singing
Compelled by the music
(A song of sorrow from long ago)
He found himself joining in harmony
Creating a beautiful
But very sad melody
Sometimes he thought
You just have to sing
Never realizing until much later
After he awoke
The other singer... was himself

Absorbed By The Sun

Her troubles and cares
At times seemed terminal
As though
There would never be
An end
A heart grown larger
By life's misfortunes
Only helped to feel
Whatever joys she sensed
To be greater
Than the terrors
She had gone through
Much in the way
Sunshine pushes out night
Suspicion and fear
Always gave way to hope
While in the end
Her darkness
Was absorbed by the sun

Woodstock Mornings

The reservoir sparkled
While dancing with the sun
As they walked hand in hand
Along the well-worn path
That circled the water's edge

No sounds of city traffic
Or early mornings movement
Could be heard anywhere about
Only two voices constantly repeating
Declarations of affection

Lost within each other's eyes
Embracing each time they stopped
With buns and coffee
From the early breakfast
Completing the Catskill dawn

THE LIVELY IMAGE

(In memory of Richard Hughes)

Because of you
My mind ponders
Half-inch rivers
That run forever
In distant lands
Where bridges are made
Of watermelon sugar
In which all things
Were done
Food that was cooked
Had lots of carrots
And lambs
Were in the flowers
And as Pauline said
That was the end
To the story

WHEN WATER CRACKS

The cold north winds
Played up and down the reservoir
As over the winter days
Thin layers of ice began to form
Each day she would walk
Along the water's edge
Thinking of him
With only a reflection
Momentarily looking back

She had grown to love
The brisk winds
And the cold falling snow
But stilled longed
For the cool warm days of spring
When he would return
And together they would watch
The melting ice
Until the water cracked

In The Third Person

Are you having an affair she asked?
The response was a quick yes
Do you love her?
Again he said yes
Do you see her often?
As much as possible came the reply
Do I know who she is?
Yes you do he said
Will you tell me… please?
……….. It's you!

I Have Never Not Seen

I've never seen
A field in bloom
That could not make
A robin sing

I've never known
A winter's day
That wasn't better
For the spring

I've never felt
A sweeter touch
Or eyes so dark
They were blinding

I've never seen
Or felt true love
That could not make
A plain man king

Changing Gears

The rustling of the trees
Drew me to the window
As the peaceful sound of the wind
Made me sway
With the gently moving branches
It had been a long while
Since I took the time
To enjoy mornings beauty
And free myself
From thoughts of work
Grabbing a cup of coffee
I sat down looking out
Sipping my hot drink
Letting the beautiful sound
Enfold me
In a peace I had not felt
For quite sometime

Bungee Jumping

The ground never came near
When I jumped from the cliff
It was the sky that fell away

Making Sense

Through the years
His hearing
Slowly diminished
In time
The world had become
A quieter place
Even his answers
Became uncomplicated
They all
Boiled down
To one word
… Huh?

Puss In Boots

I loved it
When she walked naked
Into the bedroom
Only wearing
Her hiking boots
Kind of reminded me
Of a children's
Bedtime story
… Well… sort of

Youth As I Recall

Behold a star sits by the sun
And lays a light on deeds past done
Thoughts I have since long resigned
Of seashell turtles lost in time
Recalling feelings laid to rest
Of women pure with small bared chests
That call out offers in response
And cast their eyes in nonchalance
What chance has one as fool as I
To let these memories go on by

In The Eyes Of The Young

Not fully sixteen
Her vision limited
By the steps she takes
With a bouncing gait
And an impish smile
That could only be found
On one so young
The world is so very new
With all its troubles
And problems so far ahead
It has not found her
Quite yet

SNOW CAT

Darting over the road
Like a meandering mound of snow
On a warm autumn's day
A jittery white cat
Pursuing its next meal
Zigzagged
Through the trees and grass
As it faded out of sight

After awhile
One could see
A small white dot
Disappearing
Looking like the first
Snowflake of winter
Peacefully vanishing
Into the wooded countryside

My Grandfather's Eyes

Looking at himself in the mirror
He realized he was much older now
Nowhere on his body could he find
A trace of the young man he once was
Bringing his head close to the mirror
And staring deep into his own eyes
He searched for a sign of the youth
That once smiled back at him
For a long period of time
He stood before himself
Realizing
That the kind, soft eyes
That returned his gaze
Were the same eyes
His grandfather once used
When he looked at him as a boy

www.ingramcontent.com/pod-product-compliance
Lightning Source LLC
LaVergne TN
LVHW021806060526
838201LV00058B/3251